Viking-Age Communities: *Pap*-Names and *Papar* in the Hebridean Islands

Kristján Ahronson

BAR British Series 450
2007

Published in 2016 by
BAR Publishing, Oxford

BAR British Series 450

Viking-Age Communities: Pap-*Names and* Papar *in the Hebridean Islands*

ISBN 978 1 4073 0162 4

© K Ahronson and the Publisher 2007

The author's moral rights under the 1988 UK Copyright,
Designs and Patents Act are hereby expressly asserted.

All rights reserved. No part of this work may be copied, reproduced, stored,
sold, distributed, scanned, saved in any form of digital format or transmitted
in any form digitally, without the written permission of the Publisher.

BAR Publishing is the trading name of British Archaeological Reports (Oxford) Ltd.
British Archaeological Reports was first incorporated in 1974 to publish the BAR
Series, International and British. In 1992 Hadrian Books Ltd became part of the BAR
group. This volume was originally published by Archaeopress in conjunction with
British Archaeological Reports (Oxford) Ltd / Hadrian Books Ltd, the Series principal
publisher, in 2007. This present volume is published by BAR Publishing, 2016.

Printed in England

BAR titles are available from:

              BAR Publishing
              122 Banbury Rd, Oxford, OX2 7BP, UK
EMAIL   info@barpublishing.com
PHONE +44 (0)1865 310431
FAX   +44 (0)1865 316916
              www.barpublishing.com

TABLE OF CONTENTS

ACKNOWLEDGEMENTS — i

LIST OF ILLUSTRATIONS, TABLES AND ABBREVIATIONS — iii

INTRODUCTION — 1-4

CHAPTER ONE
Pap-names and the Norse — 5-16

CHAPTER TWO
Looking to the Hebrides — 17-20

CHAPTER THREE
Pab(b)ay island names — 21-66

CHAPTER FOUR
Viking-Age communities? — 67-72

CONCLUSIONS AND FURTHER PROBLEMS — 73

REFERENCES — 74-76

ACKNOWLEDGEMENTS

General

I give thanks to Miss Lowri Angharad Hughes, Professor William Gillies, Dr Andy Dugmore, Dr Fraser Hunter and Alex Woolf as well as Prof Barry Cunliffe and Prof Ian Ralston for their advice, vision, criticisms and steadfast support. Peder Gammeltoft provided much specialist advice and has kindly commented on a draft. Exceptionally, he has recently turned his own pen to the subject and kept me abreast of this work.

Introduction

Dr Jonathan Henderson helpfully contributed his specialist knowledge of bird migrations to the ideas of the introduction.

Chapter Three

The name inventory in this chapter was possible thanks to Dr Barbara Crawford and Professor Ian Simpson's invitation to undertake this task as part of their Scottish Papar Project – I am grateful for this and especially to Dr Simon Taylor for his guidance.

Rachel Craig helpfully translated Neil Morrison's Gaelic poetry (included under Pabbay (HAR)) and I am happy to thank, for their advice and assistance, Dr Arne Kruse, Dr Ian Fraser, Ian Fisher of the RCAHMS, and Chris Fleet of the NLS Map Library.

LIST OF ILLUSTRATIONS, TABLES AND ABBREVIATIONS

Illustrations

Illustr 1 The travels of the Irish *peregrini* in the fifth to eighth centuries and the settlements and monasteries which they founded. Taken from Cunliffe (2001: 472).

Illustr 2 Distribution of *Pap*-names across Atlantic Scotland. Hebridean *Pap*-island names are indicated in red. Note the *pap*-element occurs both further south (e.g. Mull, Man) and north, in the Faroe Islands and Iceland. Adapted from map circulated at 15 March 2003 Scottish *Papar Project* meeting in St Andrews.

Illustr 3 Detail of Kinnaird's 1783 estate plan – the arrow locates *Papies Holm*.

Illustr 4 Pab(b)ay islands studied. Top: Pabbay (Harris). Middle left: Pabbay (Strath). Middle right: Pabay (South Uist). Bottom: Pabbay (Barra). Reproduced from Landranger® 18, 31 and 32, 1:50000 scale by permission of Ordnance Survey. © Crown copyright. All rights reserved. Licence number 100020276.

Tables

Table 1 Listing of *Pap*-names from Iceland, the Faroe Islands, Scotland, NW England and the Isle of Man. Potentially recent names are represented by +, while **?** notes an unclear derivation. This list draws substantially upon the work of Peder Gammeltoft and Aidan MacDonald (Gammeltoft 2004b: 36-7; MacDonald 2002: 26-9).

Table 2 Conjugation of Old Norse masculine singular noun *papi*.

Table 3 *Pap*-name forms. The ?> notation symbolises a problematic, though possible derivation. The forms *Paparey and *Paparbýli are theoretically possible, but only theoretically so: they have never been recorded in old sources. Furthermore, it is unclear to which extent indications of singular or plural are relevant, expecially if these toponymic forms came to be used as a fixed phrase (i.e. outside the grammar of word composition).

Table 4 Pab(b)ay island names, not including surrounding area names. Names are classified as **G** (Gaelic), **SSE** (Scottish Standard English), **N** (Norse), **[N]** (Norse names incorporated into G or SSE construction), **N?** (probable Norse) and **?** (uncertain).

Table 5 Preliminary survey of Pab(b)ay names derived from Norse. Numbers are approximate and exclude marine features. Note that names which derive directly from Norse (i.e. coined by Norse-speakers) are separated out from those younger names which contain Norse loan-words in Gaelic, and were therefore coined by Gaelic-speakers. This analysis was carried out by Simon Taylor.

Abbreviations

RCAHMS Royal Commission on the Ancient and Historical Monuments of Scotland

NLS National Library of Scotland

INTRODUCTION

Sculpted stones and carvings in caves and rock faces testify to an unexplored facet of early Christianity across a zone stretching from the Scottish coasts to Iceland. Though recent work paves the way for a more nuanced interpretation of this material, key uncertainties pose significant hurdles for scholarship. This book highlights the ambiguities surrounding Viking-Age Scandinavian and early Christian communities (called *papar* by later Norse literature[1]), and focuses upon the *Pap*-place-names of the north Atlantic islands in order to shed new light on our understanding of the relationships between the peoples of this zone in the early medieval period.

To elaborate, a flowering of Gaelic monasticism is well-established for the early medieval period, with individuals and monastic foundations of the 'Irish school' penetrating large areas of Europe (illustration 1) and contemporary authors such as Dicuil[2] (Tierney 1967) and Adomnán (Anderson & Anderson 1991; Sharpe 1995) providing descriptions of the north Atlantic arm of this expansion. In this way, journeys into the Ocean probably did occur and, given the clearly documented impulse to seek a *desert* (or wilderness) (Charles-Edwards 1976; Wooding 2000), exploration of the northern seas may have been spurred by a variety of catalysts, perhaps including straightforward observation of migratory bird routes[3] (Cunliffe 2002: 119). However, in spite of (1) Dicuil's and Adomnán's accounts, (2) the claims of Ari fróði and the other writers of the medieval *Íslendingabók* and *Landnámabók*, and (3) the early (but problematic) proposals by scholars such as Eugène Beauvois (Beauvois 1875)[4], the extent and character of these northern settlements is very poorly understood – as is their

---

[1] For instance, see descriptive passages in *Íslendingabók*, *Landnámabók* and *Historia Norvegiae* (*Íslendingabók*: ch 1; *Landnámabók*: ch 1; Benediktsson 1968: 4-5, 31-2; Pálsson & Edwards 1972: 14; *Historia*: ch 6; Phelpstead 2001: ch 6; Ekrem & Mortensen 2003: 64-7).

[2] Dicuil describes an early Christian community of Gaels in what appears to be the Faroe Islands (which he claims was settled c. AD 725) and a journey to Iceland by two clerics in AD 795 (Tierney 1967: 72-7).

[3] Though the migratory routes of birds are subject to rapid evolutionary change (Weidensaul 1999: 48-50), modern-day examples which travel the airways between Iceland and Scotland include the Barnacle Goose (*Branta leucopsis*) and Pink-footed Goose (*Anser brachyrhynchus*) (Jonsson 1999: 78, 84).

[4] See, however, Daniel Wilson's seminal *The Archaeology and Prehistoric Annals of Scotland* for a less problematic early discussion (Wilson 1851: 483-6).

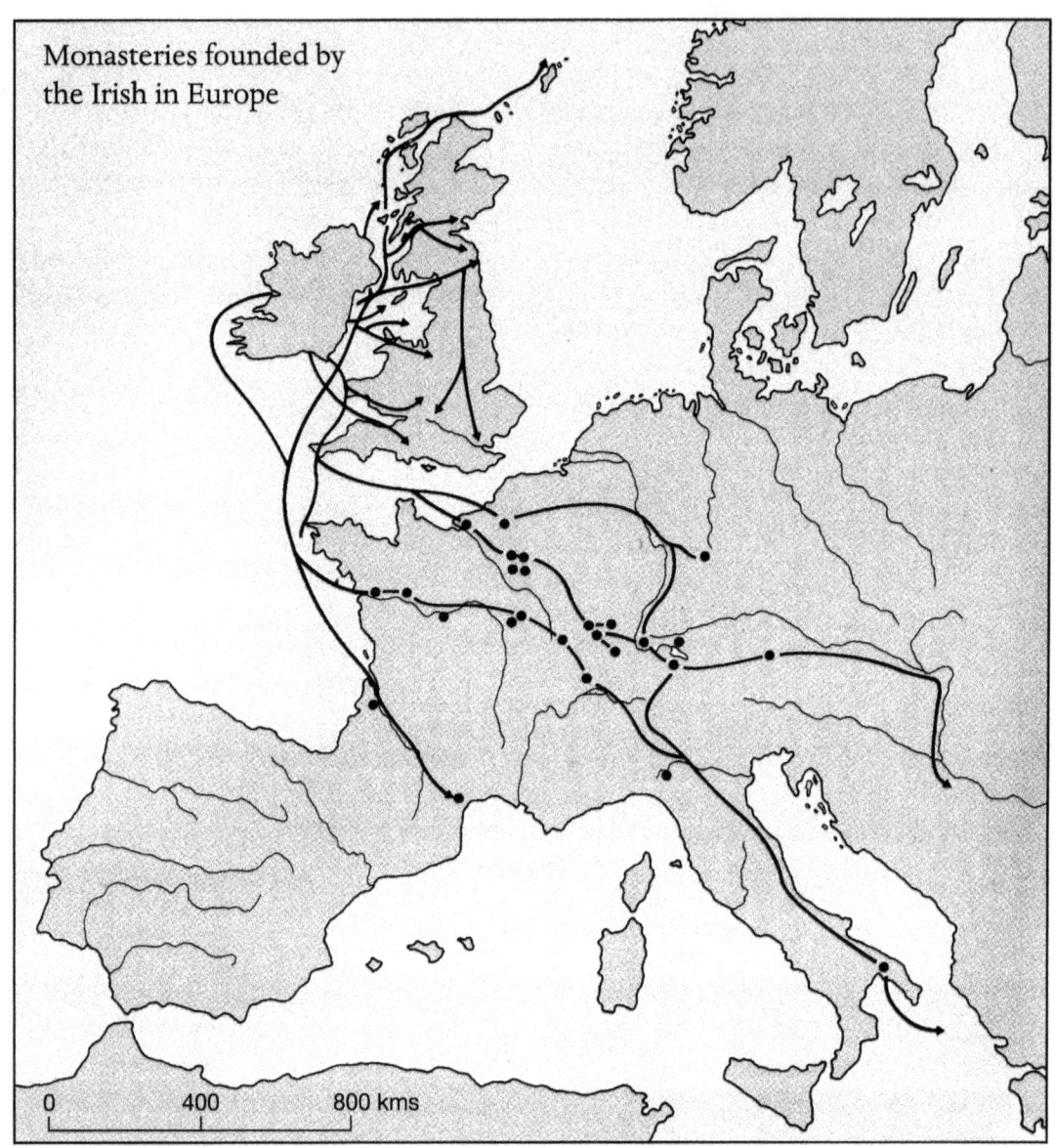

Illustr 1 The travels of the Irish *peregrini* in the fifth to eighth centuries and the settlements and monasteries which they founded. Taken from Cunliffe (2001: 472).

relationship to the Viking-Age Scandinavians who came to dominate this region by the ninth or early tenth-centuries.

In short, the idea of early Christian settlement across the north Atlantic islands was sparked long ago by study of medieval texts such as those authored by Adomnán, Dicuil and Ari fróði – and was fuelled by complementary material from other fields, such as the distribution of *pap*-element place-names across the region. Norse and Celtic scholarship have approached this material differently. A Celtic literature perspective identifies early Christian writers such as Dicuil to be operating within a coherent tradition. For instance, Jonathan Wooding provides a recent survey of the "historical context of voyaging by monastic *peregrini* in the Atlantic between c.560 and 800 AD" (Wooding 2000: 227), while Thomas O'Loughlin investigates what stories of such journeys may have symbolised for their intended audiences (O'Loughlin 1999). Importantly, what Dicuil describes as contemporary journeys into the Ocean are consistent with Thomas Charles-Edwards' investigation of the attested historical phenomenon of the *peregrinatio* drive within Irish society, in some cases to find a *desert place* in the Ocean (Charles-Edwards 1976). The situation is different with late medieval Norse literature, where unusual descriptions of *papar / papæ* (an Old Norse word) may be gathered together and contrasted with the early Christian literature of Dicuil and Adomnán. From a Norse perspective, then, the *papar* passages are exotic and lack the three-dimensionality of the Celtic literature on this topic[5].

Considering these contrasting and fundamental ambiguities, we are fortunate that recent developments – in several fields – make a broad north Atlantic characterising of the early medieval period possible and desirable. This new work includes for instance: linguistic and place-name research on Scandinavian-Gaelic contact (Gammeltoft 2004a); catalogues such as of Scotland's west-coast cross sculpture (Fisher 2001); and studies considering the role of early Christian communities in the agricultural development of Scotland's Northern Isles (Simpson & Guttman 2002) as well as of the earliest cereal cultivation in the Faroe Islands (Edwards et al. submitted). In order to draw together strands of work on archaeological, Celtic and palaeoenvironmental materials, however, problems cross-cutting the integration of these materials must first be dealt with. The present work therefore explores the toponymy of *Pap*-names (which have been associated with settlements of the aforementioned *papar*), with a case study of Hebridean *Pap*-islands.

---

[5] For instance, see Barbara Crawford's *The Papar in the North Atlantic* (Crawford 2002).

CHAPTER ONE
Pap-names and the Norse

"Most importantly ... the rarely occurring OI [Old Irish] *papa* (or *pupu*) is used to describe persons in relation to their monastic or anchorite activities in the Scottish Isles. The word occurs e.g. in the Martyrology of Oengus the Culdee, apparently composed around 828-830, but only surviving in a number of 16th-century transcriptions. In one of these versions we learn that:

> *Nem macc hui Birn do Dail Birn i n-Osraige 7 comarba Enna Arné ocus is hé sin in papa atberar do bith i n-Arainn*
> Nem moccu Birn of the Dál Birn of Ossory and successor of Enda of Aran; and he is that **papa** who is said to be in Aran

If the dating of this document is correct, a Gaelic origin for ON *papi*, m., is very conceivable."[6]

"Place-names are created by utilising the word material available at any given point in time ... by means of the standard utilisation of the syntax, grammar and vocabulary which exists as the source language at the time and place of naming. Therefore, it is possible, if enough is known about the language at the time of naming, to make an etymological analysis of the generic form of a place-name. The etymological analysis of place-names has traditionally been the main concern of all place-name researchers. However, it can be argued that this type of research deals not with place-names but with the components of place-names prior to place-name formation. [Nonetheless, subjecting place-names to an etymological analysis] ... is most helpful in trying to get to grips with how a name formation was applied, not only in its physical surroundings, but also by the society in which it was applied."[7]

Peder Gammeltoft

For well over a hundred years, Old Norse *Pap*-names and medieval *papar/papae* descriptions have been used to suggest early Christian migration(s) across the north Atlantic islands. Critical review, however, highlights still-unexplored avenues for toponymic study of *Pap*-names – and suggests more complex and nuanced interpretations of the material. A place-name denotes a location and, for the namer, articulates meaning given to that place. *Pap*-names, such as those derived from Old Norse (ON) **Papa(r)ey*, are found across a northern region incorporating the Scottish islands, Faroe Islands and Iceland. Previously, the argument has appeared straightforward: *Pap*-names describe settlements of early Christian Gaels, called *papar* by the Norse. I suggest this argument is simplistic and lacks critical rigour.

---

[6] (Gammeltoft 2004b: 41; MacDonald 1977: 26; 2002: 15-7) The Old Irish text is taken from MS Rawlinson B505.
[7] (Gammeltoft 2001: 17-8)

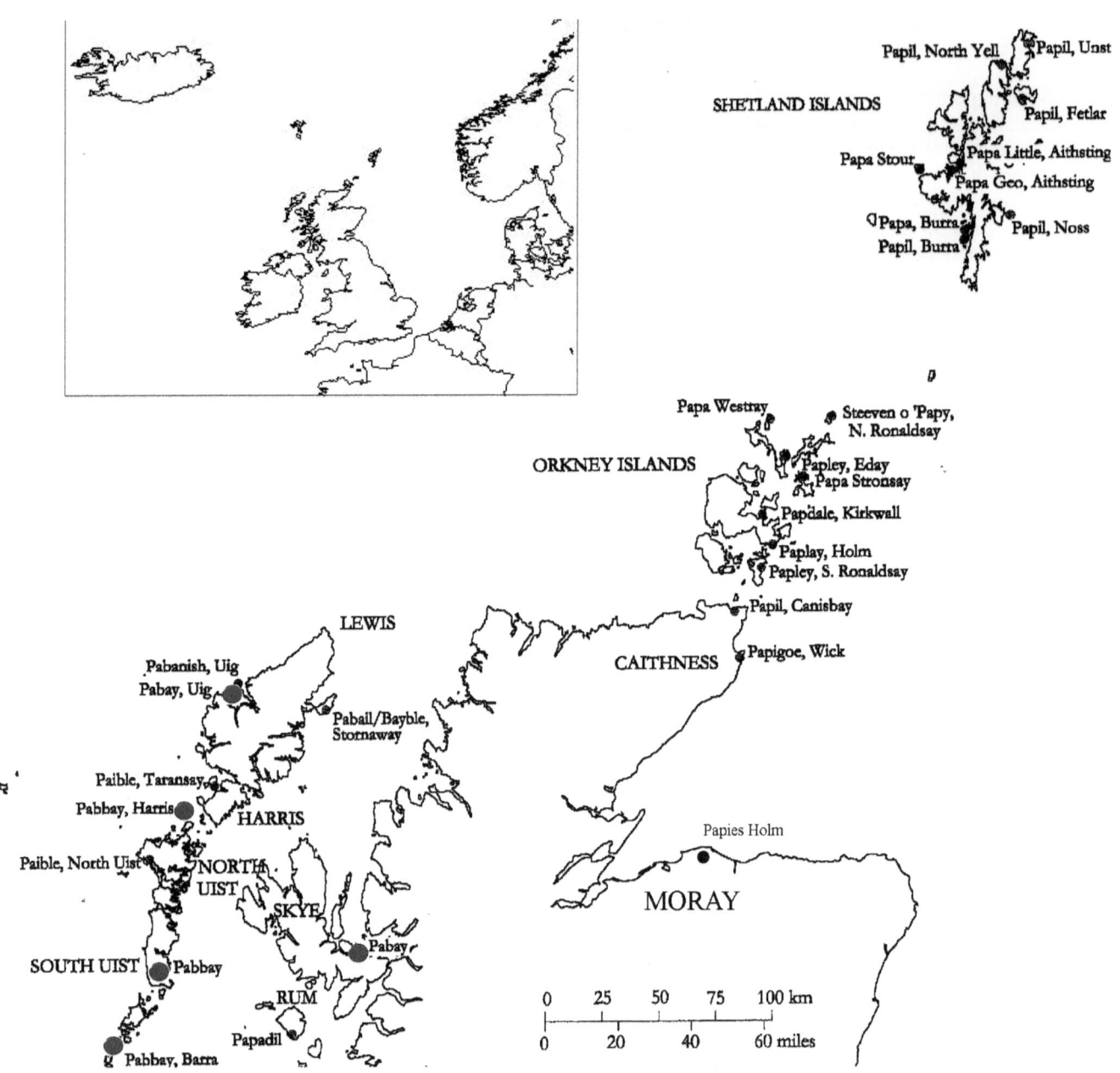

Illustr 2 Distribution of *Pap*-names across Atlantic Scotland. Hebridean *Pap*-island names are indicated in grey. Note the *pap*-element occurs both further south (e.g. Mull, Man) and north, in the Faroe Islands and Iceland. Adapted from map circulated at 15 March 2003 Scottish *Papar Project* meeting in St Andrews.

Pap-names are most common in Atlantic Scotland (see illustration 2), where *pap*-scholarship is dominated by studies of the Northern Isles. The Hebrides, notable as a core area for these names, represent a striking gap in scholarship: *Pap*-names there are little studied and have not been integrated with Northern Isles-driven work. If *Pap*-names are indeed related to early Christian Gaels, then this should be most clearly seen in these western islands, where sculpture, surviving structures, and contemporary literature identify early Christian communities. Original research was undertaken in order to rigorously assess such a relationship: this book highlights the little-studied Hebridean *Pap*-islands and presents a *toponymic inventory*[8] to underpin my conclusions. While the work of collecting this data was designed as a preliminary to place-name study on a wider front, it also serves to illuminate our specific problem – the postulated relationship between *Pap*-names, communities of early Christian Gaels and Norse colonists.

WIDER PROBLEM: What does the distribution of Pap-names across the European north Atlantic reveal?
KEY QUESTION: What do Pap-names in the Hebrides reveal about early Christian communities and the Norse?

Pap-names are found in a number of places across the north Atlantic region and, as mentioned above, they are most common in Atlantic Scotland. Table 1 lists these sites by country and region while illustration 2 plots most Scottish names – including the new discovery of *Papies Holm* (Duffus parish, Moray) (Simon Taylor, *pers. comm.*). This *Papies Holm* could be significant, as its occurrence pushes the area of these names southwards into the Moray Firth. Such an extension is both plausible and exciting, as that region has an early Christian inheritance and the Norse period there is imperfectly grasped. Additionally, table 1 presents *Kilphobull*, a recently identified *Pap*-name from the parish of Kilninian and Kilmore on the Isle of Mull. Potentially derived from Gaelic *cill* 'cell, church' + ON **Papabýli*, this name is a welcome addition to the Hebridean corpus (Gammeltoft 2001: 301).

The geographical distribution of *Pap*-names is notable: these names appear to be largely restricted to the Scottish littoral zones and archipelagos, and to the northern archipelagos of the Faroe Islands and Iceland. The Hebrides may be seen as a core area for these names albeit the least studied. The present work seeks to remedy this scholarly deficit by focusing primarily on these western islands.

---

[8] Simon Taylor guided much of the name collecting for Chapter Three, under the auspices of Barbara Crawford's and Ian Simpson's Scottish *Papar Project*. Correspondingly, a significant amount of the data was included in an unpublished project report (Ahronson 2002). That report was preliminary and I have since continued work on this data; thus the 'project material' incorporated into the present study has benefited from further analyses. (For instance, by incorporating final comments from Simon Taylor's unpublished accompanying report (Taylor 2002), as well as my own analysis and the new work of scholars such as Peder Gammeltoft (Gammeltoft 2001; 2003; 2004a; 2004b).)

At present, the name is not found in Ireland nor Scandinavia, though certain Scottish and Norwegian names, of another type, betray surface similarities to our group. This other type includes names such as the *Paps of Jura* (Jura, western Scotland) or *Papper/på Papøy* (Østfold, southeastern Norway), and have been set apart as they are pretty certainly different from ON *papa(r)* names. To elaborate, the Østfold *Papper/på Papøy* is usually understood in terms of the Norwegian word *pappe* 'breast, teat'; and the island's topography strongly suggests this meaning (Gammeltoft 2004b: 38 n1). Discussing the possibility that the north Atlantic *Pap*-names do not contain ON *papa(r)*, but share a common etymology with the Østfold name, Gammeltoft concludes that deriving these names from ON *pap 'breast, teat' is difficult to support:

> Formally, there is no reason why this possibility should not lie behind some *Pap*- place-names in the North Atlantic either. I must, however, immediately concede that I have not been able to find any suitable breast-shaped formations on or near any of the localities, apart from possibly *Papa Little* in Shetland which has a tendency to a double-peaked profile[9]. So, although ON *pap- 'breast, teat' might be a formal possibility, the topography seems to speak against this in most cases. (Gammeltoft 2004b: 38 n1)

Topography then, may be used to distinguish ON **Papa(r)ey* and **Papa(r)býli* names from names containing the Old Norse (or (Northern) Old English) word for 'breast, teat'.

---

[9] This is not to say that 'breast, teat' names need refer to paired 'paps': consider *Pap of Glencoe* (one peak) or *Paps of Jura* (three peaks).

Country/Region	*Pap*-name(s)
Iceland	*Papey* (island, S-Múlasýsla) *Papafjörður* (firth, A-Skaftafellssýsla) *Papós/*Papafjarðarós* (confluence, A-Skaftafellssýsla) *Papýli* (lost settlement) *Papi* (pool in the river Laxá) *Papafell* (mountain, Strandasýsla) +*Papakross* (cliff-face carving, Hetta, Vestmannaeyjar) +*Papahellir* (cave, A-Rangárvallasýsla)
Faroe Islands	*Paparókur* (cliff-ledges, Vestmanna) ?*Papurshálsur* (cliff-ledge, Saksun)[10]
Scotland 1: Shetland	*Papa Geo* (creek, Aithsting) *Papa Little* (island, Aithsting) *Papa Stour* (island, Sandness) *Papa* (island, Burra) *Papil Geo* (creek, Noss) *Papil Water* (loch, Fetlar) *Papil* (settlement, Burra) *Papil* (settlement, North Yell) *Papil* (settlement, Unst)
Scotland 2: Orkney	*Papa Stronsay* (island, Stronsay) *Papa Westray* (island, Westray) *Papdale* (settlement, Kirkwall and St Ola) *Papley* (district and settlement, South Ronaldsay) +*Papleyhouse* (settlement, Eday) *Ward of Papley* (mound, Holm) ?*Steeven o'Papy* (sea rock, North Ronaldsay)
Scotland 3: Caithness	*Papel* (tidal rock, Canisbay) *Papigoe* (creek and district, Wick)
Scotland 4: Moray	*Papies Holm* (settlement, Duffus parish)
Scotland 5: Hebrides	*Bayble/Paibal* (settlement, Stornoway, Lewis) *Pabanish* (rocky hill, Uig, Lewis) *Pabay* (island, Strath, Skye) *Pabay Beag* (island, Uig, Lewis) *Pabay Mór* (island, Uig, Lewis) *Pabbay* (island, Barra) *Pabbay* (island, Harris) *Pabbay* (two islands, South Uist) *Paible* (chapel and settlement, North Uist) *Paible* (chapel and settlement, Taransay) *Papadil* (islets, Rhum) *Kilphobull* (Kilninian and Kilmore parish, Mull)[11]
Man	?*Glenfaba* (Peel)
Scotland/England: Dumfries and Galloway/Cumberland	?*Papy Ha'* (Minnigaff, Kirkcudbright) ?*Papcastle* (settlement, Cumberland)

Table 1 Listing of *Pap*-names from Iceland, the Faroe Islands, Scotland, NW England and the Isle of Man. Potentially recent names are represented by +, while ? notes an unclear derivation. This list draws substantially upon the work of Peder Gammeltoft and Aidan MacDonald (Gammeltoft 2004b: 36-7; MacDonald 2002: 26-9).

---

[10] Christian Matras argued that the name *Papurshálsur* is derived from an original **Papýlishálsur* – and thus related to a now-lost *Papýli*-name in the Saksun area. He proposes first a loss of -i- from **Papýlis-*, resulting in **Papýls-*. Next, the dipthong -ý- 'uj' becomes -u- 'u'. The final change is that of -uls- to -urs-, thus **Papuls-* > *Papurs-*, producing the recorded *Papurshálsur* (Matras 1934: 187).

[11] Gammeltoft derives this name from Gaelic *cill* 'cell, church' + ON **Papabýli* (Gammeltoft 2001: 301). Alternatively, this name could relate to OI *popul* (itself derived from Latin *populus*) meaning 'people, tribe' or in modern Gaelic 'congregation, especially Catholic' (cf *Cairnpapple* in Lanarkshire).

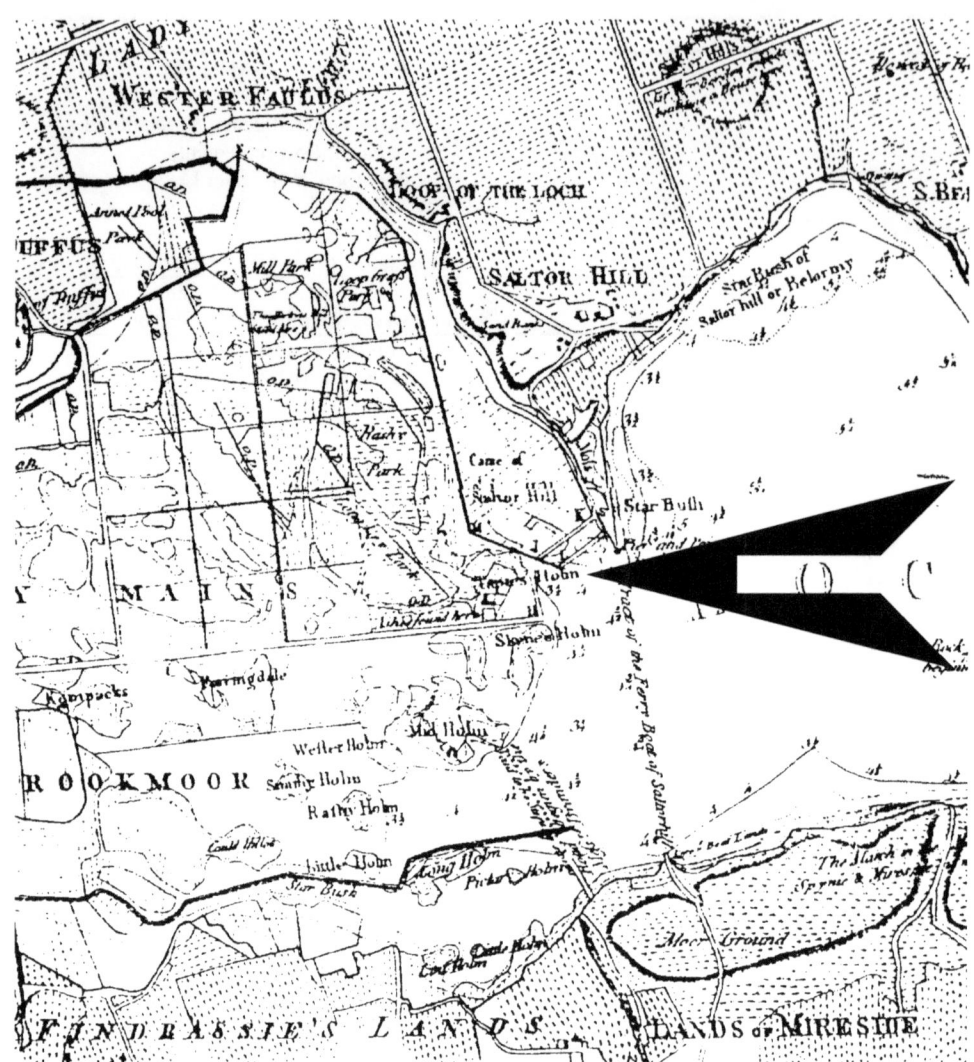

Illustr 3 Detail of Kinnaird's 1783 estate plan – the arrow locates *Papies Holm*[12].

---

[12] In its modern form, *Papies Holm* has a Scots English plural morpheme. The Scots English ending of *Papies* should not be seen as a difficulty for identifying *Papies Holm* as a north Atlantic *Pap*-name, however, as morphological morphemes are rather unstable and often 'updated' to new linguistic conditions, such as internal language-structural changes as well as language change (Sandnes 2003: 291-2).

The name is identified in illustration 3 on an eighteenth-century estate plan detail. *Papies Holm* (NJ203665) is one of several *holm*-names given to islets on the west shore of the Loch of Spynie (Simon Taylor, *pers. comm.*). A number of minor place-names from estates in Spynie, Drainie, St Andrews-Lhanbryde and Duffus are recorded on this 1783 map, titled "Map of the Loch of Spynie and adjacent Grounds. Surveyed by Authority of the Right Hon. The Lords of Council and Session. And agreeable to Instruction from Sir William Gordon of Gordonstown, Baronet, Alex. Brander of Kinnedder and John Brander of Pitgaveny Esq. by Hugh Kinnaird" (Keillar 1994: fig 5).

Ian Keillar gives the following discussion of the former extent of *Loch Spynie* (NJ235664):

Loch Spynie is miserably small compared to its conjectured dimensions about 1000 AD. Then there was open sea extending from west of Burghead to east of Lossiemouth, and Burghead and Kinneddar were part of an off shore island. Authorities for the above include; Peacock, Young, Mackintosh and Ross (Peacock 1968: 116; Young 1871: 5-36; Mackintosh

It is important to emphasize that *Pap*-names are Old Norse constructions. As a consequence, our exploration of the Hebridean names demands some discussion of current thinking on Scandinavian language use in Atlantic Scotland. In the Viking Age, the area of Scandinavian influence in Scotland saw two power centres emerge: one in the Northern Isles and the other in the Hebrides and Isle of Man[13]. From this time until the end of the twelfth century, a region incorporating Shetland, Orkney, Caithness, Sutherland, the Hebrides and the Isle of Man formed a common language area where Old Norse was spoken. In the Western Isles of Scotland, a form of Old Norse appears to have preceded the late medieval dominance of Gaelic there. Old Norse may have flourished in the west until the mid-thirteenth century, when the Scottish king secured authority in the Hebrides and Isle of Man (though Orkney and Shetland remained 'Scandinavian' until AD 1468-9). An unresolved question is the length of time before Gaelic completely replaced the Old Norse spoken in these western islands – the suggestion being that Hebridean Old Norse disappeared rapidly under Scottish influence. Caution to this scenario, however, are other examples of Scandinavian speech that survived changes in authority: in Orkney and Shetland the *Norn* language (derived from Old Norse) was used until the seventeenth and eighteenth centuries. The Hebridean case remains unresolved (Gammeltoft 2004a: 53-4; 2001: 23-30).

Gammeltoft has very recently published a study that investigates the transformation in the Western Isles from Old Norse to Gaelic speech. By studying Gaelic and Scandinavian phonetics, grammar, lexical loans and place-names, he is able to outline a scenario of late medieval language shift in the Hebrides. The distribution of a number of Gaelic phonetic features may result from this language shift. The devoicing in Manx and Scottish Gaelic of *b*, *d*, *g* to [b_o, d_o, g_o] (in contrast to Irish Gaelic); the initial stress on native words in Scottish Gaelic and in the Irish Gaelic dialects of Ulster and western Connaught; and the supradentalisation and retroflection of certain consonant clusters in the Hebrides are proposed to result from Scandinavian interference on Gaelic (Gammeltoft 2004a: 55-9). Similarly, large-scale Old Norse to Gaelic language shift may be reflected by the AD 900-1200 grammatical simplification in Gaelic, which appears to have been greatest in Manx and Scottish Gaelic (Gammeltoft 2004a: 60). Alongside the notable phonetic and grammatical interference, lexical loans into Gaelic are surprisingly slight (c. 200 words), though the combination of significant phonetic and grammatical interference with a small number of lexical loans fits well with models of language shift-induced interference (Gammeltoft 2004a: 61-7). The numerous Old

---

1928; Ross 1987: 19-24). The western end of this open seaway was closed by storm beaches circa 1100 and by the end of the 15th century, the Loch of Spynie was completely cut off from the sea. By the middle of the 18th century the only remaining evidence for the one time existence of a sea passage was the string of lochs and mosses as shown in ... [Kinnaird's map]. (Keillar 1994: 7)

[13] In the twelfth-century *Historia Norvegiae*, Scotland's Atlantic islands are described thus:

Que quidem diuersis incolis acculte nunc in duo regna sunt diuise: sunt enim Meridiane insule [Suðreyjar or Hebrides] *regulus sublimate, Brumales uero comitum presidio decorate, qui utrique regibus Norwegie non modica persoluunt tributa.*

They are populated by different peoples and now split into two domains; the southern isles [Suðreyjar or Hebrides] have been elevated by petty kings, the northern graced by the protection of earls, both of whom pay no mean tribute to the kings of Norway. (*Historia*: ch 5; Ekrem & Mortensen 2003: 64-5; Phelpstead 2001)

Norse place-names found in the Hebrides are also consistent with the suggestion of large-scale language shift there:

> That so many place-names of Scandinavian origin remain in existence and have not been replaced by new Gaelic place-names shows that the user-group of these place-names must have continued to live in the area. Had the Scandinavians been driven out in connection with the language change, the survival of anything but perhaps the most central names is hardly conceivable. Only continuity in the user-group could have facilitated the survival of place-names of Scandinavian origin in this number. At the same time, however, the high number of place-names also bear witness to longstanding contacts between Gaelic and Scandinavian speaking people in the area. Had Gaelic-speaking people not already accepted a great number of the place-names, the rate of survival would probably not have been as high as it is. (Gammeltoft 2004a: 71-2)

Thus the existence of such a number of Old Norse place-names suggests a continuity of user-group and longstanding contacts between Old Norse and Gaelic speakers. Additional support for this scenario is found in the limited interference of Gaelic upon the Scandinavian languages. The limited lexical loans *from* Gaelic (as the only type of Gaelic interference on the Scandinavian languages) suggest that interference in this direction was not intense and resulted from language contact through bilingualism. Furthermore, that c. 8% of these loan words serve a religious function may reflect the Christian influence of Gaelic speakers on Old Norse-speaking communities of the Atlantic area (Gammeltoft 2004a: 64, 67).

Cast against this background (or one like it), research into the *Pap*-names has fallen into three camps. Earlier scholarship has argued that these names testify to 'Irish' Christian settlements across Scotland, the Faroe Islands and Iceland *predating* the Viking Age (Beauvois 1875: 69-72). In contrast, recent years have explored the idea of late Viking Age 'antiquarianism' among the Scandinavian communities of the north Atlantic – proposing that the late Norse coining of *Pap*-names asserts (or invents) continuity with a Christian past (MacDonald 2002; Lowe 2002: 94-5). Another idea is that, though *Pap*-names are potentially related to early Christian communities of the seventh and eighth centuries, these names were given by *Norse speakers* in the early Viking Age – and thus describe '*papar*' <u>within</u> an early Norse context in the Scottish islands, Faroe Islands and Iceland (Gammeltoft 2004b: 36-41; Lamb 1995: 17-8).

Given the wide-ranging interpretations outlined above, understanding the *pap*-element is crucial to the problem of these names. As noted in the Introduction, the earliest literature to mention the *pap*-element describes *papar* or *papae* as early Christian 'Irish' in Iceland (or African Jews in Orkney) – in both cases these populations are portrayed to precede Norse settlement there and as having minimal contact with the colonists (*Íslendingabók*: ch 1; *Landnámabók*: ch 1; Benediktsson 1968: 4-5, 31-2; Pálsson & Edwards 1972: 14; *Historia*: ch 6; Ekrem & Mortensen 2003: 64-7). These twelfth- and thirteenth-century texts were written with purpose; and as I argue elsewhere (Ahronson forthcoming), this purpose is especially evident in the case of *Historia Norvegiae*'s Africans "... *judaismo adhærentes* / ... adhering to Judaism" (*Historia*: ch 6; Storm 1880: 90; Anderson 1922: 331). As for medieval traditions of early Christian settlements encountered by Scandinavians (in contrast to the lone claim of the *Historia Norvegiae*), these persisted into the modern period. The following folktale from the Faroe Islands is one such example, published in the mid-nineteenth-century:

> Quelque temps avant que les Norvégiens s'emparassent des Færeys, il s'y était établi des hommes que le narrateur considérait comme des saints, attendu qu'ils avaient la puissance de faire des signes et des miracles, de guérir les blessures et les maladies ... A l'arrivée des Norvégiens, qui étaient très-violents, quelques-uns de ces gens s'éloignèrent par mer; d'autres se réfugièrent dans des cavernes. (Beauvois 1875: 68 n1; Schrœter 1849-51: 146-7)[14]

Case	Singular form	Plural form
Nominative	papi	papar
Accusative	papa	papar
Dative	papa	pöpum
Genitive	papa	papa

Table 2 Conjugation of Old Norse masculine singular noun *papi*.

Proposed original forms	Meaning	Potential derivations
*Papaey	'island of *papi* (s.)'	Papey/Papa/Pab(b)ay
*Paparey	'island of *papar* (pl.)'	Papey/Papa/Pab(b)ay OR *Paprey > *Pabra[15] ?> Pab(b)ay
*Papaey	'island of *papar* (pl.)'	Papey/Papa/Pab(b)ay
*Papabýli	'farm of *papi* (s.)'	Papýli > Papil/Papley/Paible
*Paparbýli	'farm of *papar* (pl.)'	*Paprýli > Papýli > Papil/Papley/Paible
*Papabýli	'farm of *papar* (pl.)'	Papýli > Papil/Papley/Paible

Table 3 *Pap*-name forms. The ?> notation symbolises a problematic, though possible derivation. The forms *Paparey and *Paparbýli are theoretically possible, but only theoretically so: they have never been recorded in old sources. Furthermore, it is unclear to which extent indications of singular or plural are relevant, expecially if these toponymic forms came to be used as a fixed phrase (i.e. outside the grammar of word composition).

A belief in early Christian (Irish)[16] settlements across the early medieval north is thus of significant antiquity and longevity. *Pap*-names, understood to contain the Old Norse masculine noun *papi* (conjugated in table 2), are presumably related to descriptions of these early Christian (Irish) *papar*. In order to further understand these names, table 3

---

[14] Taken from Beauvois, though he himself extracts this folktale from Schrœter.

[15] Though the *Pabra* name-form is recorded in Forbes' *Place-Names of Skye and Adjacent Islands*, this name is puzzling: it could derive from *Paparey, but this possibility is problematic as this source is so late that to postulate the survival of a variant Old Norse form of *Pabra* would be dangerous (Forbes 1923: 272).

[16] As mentioned above, I elsewhere propose that the claim of Orkney's *papae* being "*Africanus ... judaismo adhærentes*" was politically driven rather than 'historically legitimate' – thus I shall set aside this problematic passage for the moment.

In 1995, Raymond Lamb proposed an identification for Orkney's *papar* as Roman Churchmen comparable to those of Frankish Gaul and Anglo-Saxon England (Lamb 1995: 26). However, the north Atlantic distribution of *Pap*-names, incorporating Scotland's Western Isles, instead suggests an association with the northwards-looking Church of the Scottish west.

outlines proposed original forms, meaning and potential derivations for *Pap*-island and *Pap*-farm names.

These proposed original forms and derivations need elaboration. The case of *Papaey > *Papey/Papa/Pab(b)ay* is simple: the medial vowel (*Pap<u>a</u>ey*) is lost owing to Old Norwegian syncope[17], resulting in the *Papey/Papa/Pab(b)ay* forms. The alternate derivation of *Paparey > *Pabra > *Pab(b)ay* is problematic because, after syncope, the uncommon sound combination [-pr-] remains nonetheless possible in Old Norse – thus the loss of [-r-] in **Pab<u>r</u>a* > *Pab(b)ay* cannot be understood as a straightforward sound change. The *Paparey > *Paprey > *Pabra > *Pab(b)ay* derivation must therefore be considered unlikely, whereas the proposed *Papaey > *Papey/Papa/Pab(b)ay* is plausible.

On the other hand, the case of **Papa(r)býli* > **Paprýli/Papýli* > *Papil/Papley/Paible* is less clear. Again, the medial vowel (*Pap<u>a</u>(r)býli*) is lost owing to Old Norwegian syncope. The initial [b-] in *býli* is also lost, here because of phonotaxis: a pronunciation of the [-pb-] in **Pa<u>pb</u>ýli* is not permitted according to the set of allowed sequences of speech sounds in Old Norse. Similarly, the [-prb-] in **Pa<u>prb</u>ýli* is very problematic, so in this instance the [-rb-] would also be dropped. For the -*býli* name then, either proposed original form of *Papabýli or *Paparbýli is possible, though *Papabýli is preferable by analogy with *Papaey (Gammeltoft, *pers. comm.*).

Thus *Papaey and *Papabýli are the preferred original forms, though *Paparbýli is also possible. As may be seen in table 2, both singular *papi* and plural *papa* are identical in this conjugation; therefore the *Papaey and *Papabýli names may denote either '*papi* island' and '*papi* farm' or '*papar* island' and '*papar* farm' – or some combination of these.

In his 2002 study of *papar* names, Aidan MacDonald noted that ON *papi* is usually understood to be a borrowing from Old Irish (which itself draws upon a Latin original); he cites F W Wainwright, Hermann Pálsson, Paul Edwards and A O Anderson as supporting this Irish origin (MacDonald 2002: 15; Wainwright 1962: 100; Pálsson & Edwards 1972: 15 n3; Pálsson 1955: 120-2; Anderson 1922: 341 n2). However, MacDonald also suggests the possibility of a Germanic source (also derived from Latin *papa*) for ON *papi* (MacDonald 2002: 17). Accepting a Latin source, Gammeltoft has assessed potential Germanic and Old Irish origins for the Old Norse use of *papi* in the sense of 'cleric or Christian'. Gammeltoft proposes that a Germanic origin for the specifically north Atlantic meaning 'cleric or Christian' is highly problematic, since Old English *pāpa*, Old High German *pabes*, and East Frisian *pape*, *pâp* were used solely for 'Pope', and that 'Pope' is the meaning of Old Danish *papa* or *pave* and Old Norwegian *pafi* or *papi*. It may be countered that Middle Low German *pape* did develop the meaning cleric, but that this is late[18] and the first mainland Scandinavian use of the

---

[17] This syncope (or vowel resolution/vowel simplification) was also active in Old Icelandic, though to a lesser degree than in Old Norwegian. Gammeltoft discusses many of these linguistic points in relation to *Pap*-names (Gammeltoft 2004b: 41-2). This syncope may be chronologically constrained and the implications of this will be returned to later, in the results and discussion section.

[18] Beauvois provides an example of this late medieval Germanic usage of the word:

> C'est en effet dans le sens que le mot *papa* est employé dans la *Poëme Frison* (Thet Freske Riim, vers 1476), chronique rimée en vieux frison, publié par la Société provinciale Frisonne (Workum 1835: 49, 81). (Beauvois 1875: 70 n3)

word to describe a 'cleric' is the fifteenth-century Swedish *pape* (Gammeltoft 2004b: 39-40).

Alternatively, the north Atlantic meaning of 'cleric or Christian' may be compared with the Old High German *phafo* 'priest, especially lower clergy', which C-E Thors derives from an ultimately Greek rather than Latin origin. Thors proposes that Old High German *phafo* is a loan from Gothic, where *papan* occurs in the Gothic calendar fragment[19], and is itself ultimately drawn from Greek παπᾶς, which in the fourth century held the meaning 'clericus minor' and was easily distinguished from πάπας 'Pope'. Thors suggests both the Greek παπᾶς and πάπας "*egentigen tillhört barnspråket* / belonged to the sphere of children's language" (Thors 1957: 37-8); he also derives Old Slavic *popu* from Greek παπᾶς. Thus it may be that Old High German *phafo* (attested in Middle High German *phaffe* Middle Low German *pape*, Old Frisian *papa* and Middle Dutch *pape*, all in the sense of 'priest, spiritual') has a Greek rather than Latin origin. However, the word is largely absent from the Nordic languages, occurring only once in the Old Swedish poem *Tio Guds bud*[20], though this poem includes many "*norvagismer* / Norwagisms" and "*germanismer* / Germanisms" – Thors suspects the poem's *papa* is just one of these. According to Thors then, Old High German *phafo* cannot be demonstrated to have entered the Scandinavian languages (Thors 1957: 37-8).

In contrast to the difficulties with a Germanic derivation, an Old Irish source is straightforward: Old Irish (OI) *popa/pobba/bobba* held the meaning 'father' and was used as a respectful address (following the form *poba* + personal name), whereas the rare OI *papa* or *pupu* described monastic or anchoritic individuals (MacDonald 2002: 15-7; Gammeltoft 2004b: 40-1). As noted in this book's fronting quote, one transcription of the early ninth-century *Martyrology of Oengus the Culdee* describes Enda of Aran as just such a *papa*: "*is hé sin in papa atberar do bith i n-Arainn* / he is that papa who is said to be in Aran" (MacDonald 2002: 15; Gammeltoft 2004b: 41). Thus, rather than supporting an Old Germanic derivation, linguistic arguments suggest an Old Irish origin for the north Atlantic use of ON *papi* as 'cleric or Christian' (Gammeltoft 2004b: 41). A third possibility, still largely unexplored, is a Pictish source for ON *papi*. Such an origin is conceivable, considering that most *Pap*-names are located in what may have been Pictish-speaking areas at the outset of the Viking Age (Kruse in press). Further research along these lines is called for.

Looking to the places that *Pap*-names denote, and the way the element is used in name constructions, proves a further avenue for understanding the toponyms. Combining the *pap*-element with 'island' or 'settlement' is comparable in practice to the naming of an island using a personal name specific, as in the Shetland examples of *Hildisay* (< ON *Hildirsey 'Hildir's island') and *Trondra* (< ON *Þrondarey 'Þrondr's island'). Thus, for the namer, the *pap*-, *Hild*- and *Þrond*-element reflects the idea that *papi/papar*, *Hildir* or *Þrondr* owned or were first to settle there. In other words, "a place-name with the element *papi*, m., 'a priest, Christian' with *ey*, f., 'island' or *býli*, m., 'settlement', signals the association of a locality with the *Papar*, be it their presence at, or ownership of, the locality" (Gammeltoft 2004b: 43).

---

[19] "*I got. kalenderfragment fines vid 29.10. bi Werekan papan.* / In the Gothic calendar fragment the word is used for 29.10.: bi Werekan papan." (Thors 1957: 37-8).

[20] "*Jak troer then mann vil illa rapa; Some y wil elska prest eller papa*" (Thors 1957: 37-8).

VIKING-AGE COMMUNITIES

Following this context of ownership or settlement makes the Orkney-led claim that *Pap*-sites "are always the most fertile spots of a parish" intriguing (Fisher 2002: 45; Smith 1842: 226; Lamb 1995: 15-7). If these names are sited on the best land in a parish, does this signal a favourable role for *papar* in the local hierarchy? Or, alternatively, could these soils have been improved by *papar* through agricultural innovation? Work is ongoing to explore and refine these claims for fertile soils: initial efforts targeted the Northern Isles (Simpson & Guttman 2002), while more recent fieldwork looks to the Western Isles (Ian Simpson, *pers. comm.*).

A final area of research, only recently under scrutiny, is the dating of *Pap*-names. In 2002, MacDonald and Lowe questioned the earlier assumption that the names were coined upon the arrival of Old Norse-speaking colonists. MacDonald instead argued that the likely period for "the creation of all or most of these names is, broadly, the second half of the ninth century and the tenth, but with the overall chronological limits probably varying locally" (MacDonald 2002: 22). He posited *Pap*-names were inspired by oral and written traditions of contact-period Christian (Irish) communities – and thus coined and then applied to places in the landscape retrospectively (MacDonald 2002: 21, 24 n6). Lowe, on the other hand, suggested *Pap*-naming flourished as the twelfth-century fledgling Church "sought to attach itself to something that was much older" (Lowe 2002: 95). Gammeltoft challenges these proposals. On linguistic and toponymic grounds, he argues *Pap*-island and *Pap*-farm names were coined well before the twelfth century and, as island and generic settlement names, would typically be among the earliest Norse names in the north Atlantic area (Gammeltoft 2004b: 42-3).

In short then, *Pap*-names present a difficult area for scholars of both the early Christian Gaelic *and* Viking-Age Norse worlds. Correspondingly, when exploring the problem posed by their distribution across the European north Atlantic, the Hebrides form a natural focus. These islands were home to a number of early Christian communities and, as we have seen, strong Norse settlement. Therefore the way in which these names relate to early Christian Gaels and Norse colonists should be most clearly seen in the Hebrides – the islands where both groups are archaeologically and historically visible.

CHAPTER TWO
Looking to the Hebrides

The hypotheses assessed in this book respond to the key question: *what do Pap-names in the Hebrides reveal about early Christian communities and the Norse?* Three hypotheses explore this problem by testing ideas drawn from wider *pap*-scholarship against the Hebridean corpus of *Pap*-island names. *Pap*-islands are chosen because they represent comparable, clearly bounded areas suitable for detailed *limited* study. In future work, researchers may test ideas formulated by this study in other north Atlantic areas, or against other name types (e.g. *Pap*-farm names). As mentioned in the introduction, implicit in much earlier scholarship was the argument that *Pap*-names describe settlements of early Christian Gaels, called *papar* by the Norse[21]. An early advocate of this idea was the French scholar Eugène Beauvois (I explore his scholarship at length elsewhere (Ahronson forthcoming)). Writing in 1875, Beauvois suggested that *Pap*-names remembered early Christian Gaels in Scotland's Northern Isles and Iceland. Of the Northern Isles, he writes:

> Il n'y a, en effet, plus de restes de l'ancienne population celtique dans les Orcades; mais, bien que les Papas n'y aient pas laissé de descendants, leur nom n'a pas moins été conservé dans ceux des îles de *Papa westra* et *Papa stronsa*, et des localités de *Paplay*. Fordun, qui composa vers 1380 sa chronique d'Écosse parle d'une *Papeay tertia* dont on ne connaît pas la position. De même dans les Shetlands, il y a trois îles qui rappellent les Papas: *Papa stour* (Papey stóra), *Papa little* (Papey lítla) et *Papa*, ainsi qu'un domaine de *Papil* (Beauvois 1875: 69-70)

The following hypothesis is drawn from Beauvois, but applied to the Hebridean case: *the distribution of Pap-names reflects the settlement of early Christian Gaels before the Viking Age*[22].

---

[21] That is not to say that *all* earlier scholarship shared these ideas. Indeed, in Iceland especially, there has been criticism of the idea that *Pap*-names remember early Christian *papar*, see for instance Sveinbjarnardóttir's work (Sveinbjarnardóttir 1972; 2002: 101). Furthermore, other novel approaches to *Pap*-names have been proposed by Icelandic scholars. For example, Sturla Friðriksson suggested *Pap*-island names were given because of puffin colonies at these places – and that puffin colouring is reminiscent of priest's robes: thus the proposed original meaning for *Papey* of 'priest or puffin island' (Friðriksson 1982). However, the necessary antiquity of *papi* as an alternate name for a puffin is not established, nor does this meaning account for *Pap*-farm names or the proximity of these names to early Christian sculpture sites (Fisher 2002).

[22] One of the more recent writers to work with this idea was Gillian Fellows-Jensen, when she suggested *Pap*-names may have been applied, during Scandinavian colonisation, to sites recently abandoned by early Churchmen (Fellows-Jensen 1996: 116; Gammeltoft 2003: 44).

VIKING-AGE COMMUNITIES

In concluding the previous section, MacDonald's and Lowe's arguments for dating *Pap*-names were touched upon. MacDonald posited that the name was coined retrospectively in the late ninth to tenth centuries, while Lowe suggested the twelfth. Their arguments propose the hypothesis that: *the distribution of Pap-names reflects retrospective names given by Old Norse speakers in either the late ninth and tenth century or the twelfth century.*

The final hypothesis emerges both from the realisation that *Pap*-names are Norse constructions, and from Gammeltoft's linguistic and toponymic arguments for an early dating of the name forms. This last hypothesis proposes that: *the distribution of Pap-names reflects the character of earliest Norse settlement.*

In testing the significance and character of the *Pap*-name distribution, a toponymic inventory of four Hebridean *Pap*-islands was undertaken. On the assumption that investigating minor names qualifies studies of large-scale distributions, all names from these islands were collected and the hypotheses considered against this newly-created body of data. As mentioned earlier, the Hebrides were selected as a target area because of the strong Norse presence there and also because, if *Pap*-names are indeed related to early Christian Gaels, then this should be most clearly seen in those western islands where sculpture, surviving structures and contemporary literature identify early Christian communities.

A name catalogue is a fresh contribution to knowledge and an important early stage of toponymic research. Specifically, the production and analysis of such an inventory, alongside linguistic and toponymic arguments, permits informed consideration of the proposed hypotheses. For instance, if the inventory were to reveal an absence of Norse minor names on *Pab(b)ay* islands, then one might suggest these places did not experience Scandinavian settlement (though it must be remembered that Old Norse place-names are lucky survivals). Conversely, if inventory revealed *all* minor names as Norse, then longlasting Scandinavian settlement would need to be proposed. Alternatively, if no name patterns were shared between *Pab(b)ay* islands, then the distribution of *Pabbay* names raises more complex questions.

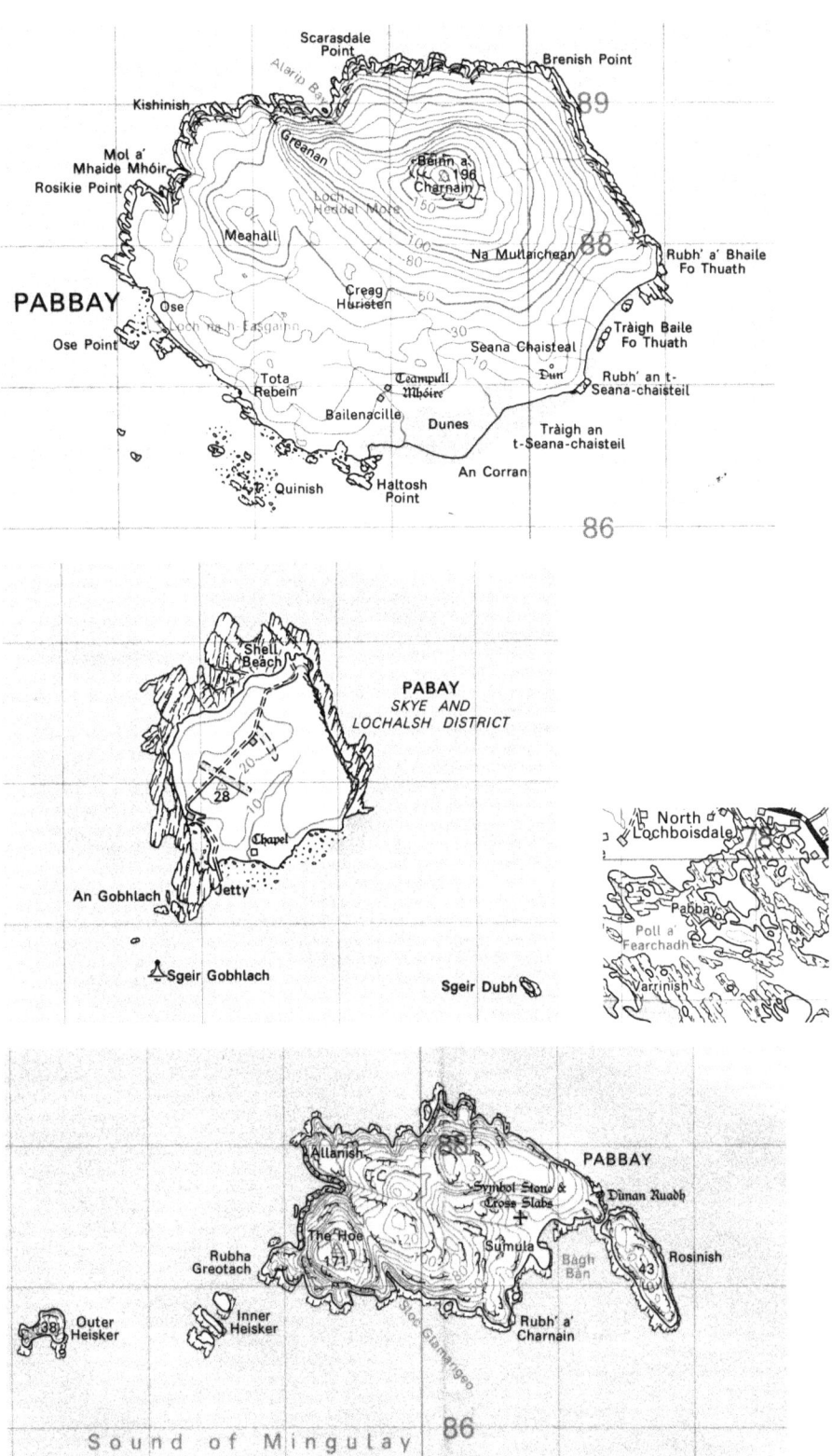

Illustr 4 Pab(b)ay islands studied. Top: Pabbay (Harris). Middle left: Pabbay (Strath). Middle right: Pabay (South Uist). Bottom: Pabbay (Barra). Reproduced from Landranger® 18, 31 and 32, 1:50000 scale by permission of Ordnance Survey. © Crown copyright. All rights reserved. Licence number 100020276.

Ordnance Survey Pathfinder, Landranger, and 6 inch first edition maps were searched alongside the historic map collection of the National Map Library of Scotland. Following the map searches, the Ordnance Survey Name Books housed in the Royal Commission for Ancient and Historic Monuments of Scotland were accessed and examined. A further stage of work involved locating and searching textual material, such as Donald MacKillop's 1991 *Sea-Names of Berneray Ainmean-Mhara Bhearnaraigh* (for Harris). Finally, oral collections housed in the School of Scottish Studies were explored. One such oral collection is the place-name list for Pabbay (Harris) recorded in 1985 (SSS PNS85/2).

Specifically, this inventory collects all place-names on four distinct Hebridean islands: Pabbay in the Sound of Harris (Harris parish), Pabbay of Loch Boisdale (two islands, South Uist parish), Pabay off Skye's Broadford Bay (Strath parish), and Pabbay of the Barra group (Barra parish)[23]. To allow easy integration into further studies (which may require island-specific sorting), each island is presented as a discrete study, including its own guide to entries, abbreviations, parish information, name inventory and references. With the exception of Pabbay (Barra), place-name entries were standardised according to a form supplied by Simon Taylor for computerised entry into the Scottish Place-Name Database. Pabbay (Barra) entries were sourced from Anke Beate Stahl's doctoral study of the Barra islands, and thus follow her alternate format (also standardised for entry into the Scottish Place-Name Database) (Stahl 1999).

---

[23] Anke Beate Stahl has produced a toponymic inventory, as yet unpublished, for Pabay Mór and Pabay Beag off Lewis (Uig parish), thus completing the Hebridean group of *Pap*-islands.

CHAPTER THREE
Pab(b)ay island names

Major and minor names were collected from *Pab(b)ay* islands in the Sound of Harris, Loch Boisdale, Broadford Bay and the Sound of Mingulay, as well as surrounding areas. This chapter catalogues these names by discrete island. Table 4 lists all island names (classified by language) and is followed by the inventory. Working from the premise that a toponymic inventory refines ideas drawn from large-scale distribution studies, multiple hypotheses were considered when interpreting the data:

- *The distribution of Pap-names reflects the settlement of early Christian Gaels before the Viking Age.*
- *The distribution of Pap-names reflects retrospective names given by Old Norse speakers in either the late ninth and tenth century or the twelfth century.*
- *The distribution of Pap-names reflects the character of the earliest Norse settlement.*

VIKING-AGE COMMUNITIES

Pabbay (HAR)	Pabay (STH)	Pabay (SUS)	Pabbay (BRR)
PABBAY **N**	PABAY **N**	PABBAY **N**	RUBHA GREOTACH **G**
ALARIP BAY **[N]**	SHELL BEACH **SSE**	WELL **SSE**	ALLANISH **N**
LINEN COVE **SSE**	FORD **SSE**		RUBH' ALAINIS **[N]**
SCARASDALE POINT **[N]**	LION ROCK **SSE**		AN CEARCALL **G**
BREMISH POINT **[N]**	CHAPEL (REMS OF) **SSE**		THE HOE **[N]**
TARRENSEY I. **[N]**	JETTY **SSE**		AN T-AONACH PABACH **G**
KISHINISH **N**	AN GOBHLACH **G**		SLOC GLANSICH **G**
MEAHALL **N**	GRAVE YARD (DISUSED) **SSE**		SLOC AN UISGE **G**
MOL A' MHAIDE MHÓIR **G**	MOSS **SSE**		SYMBOL STONE **SSE**
ROSIKIE POINT **[N?]**			SUMULA **N**
VOLRI GEO **N?**			BÀGH BÀN **G**
GREANAN **N?**			DÙNAN RUADH **G**
LOCH HEDDAL BEG **[N]**			ROSINISH **N**
LOCH HEDDAL MORE **[N]**			STEIR **N?**
LOCH HEDDAL **[N]**			LANDING PLACE **SSE**
HEDDAL **N**			CAIRNS **SSE**
LINGAY **N**			SLOC GLAMARIGEO **[N]**
BEINN A' CHARNAIN **G**			RUBH' A' CHÀRNAIN **G**
BAILE-FO-THUATH **G**			PABBAY **N**
LOCH NA H-EASGAINN **G**			BÀGH NA H-AONAICH **G**
OSE **N**			AN CNOC DUBH **G**
OSE POINT **[N]**			BOGHA CHIGEIN AN EAR **G**
BROAD RKS **SSE**			BOGHA CHIGEIN BEAG **G**
CREAG HURISTEN **[N]**			BOGHA CHIGEIN A DEAS **G**
TEAMPULL BEAG **G**			BOGHA CHIGEIN MÓR **G**
TOTA REBEIN **[N?]**			BOGHA NÉILL AN TÀILLEIR **G**
BAILE-LINGAY **G**			SGEIREAN SLOC GHLEANSAICH **G**
NA MULLAICHEAN **G**			CNOC TUATH **G**
LINGAY BURN **[N]**			CREAG **G**
RUBH' A' BHAILE FO THUATH **G**			BISHOP'S ISLES **SSE**
REEF **SSE**			BOGHANNAN AN RUBHA PHABAICH **G**
GINNOCH **?**			RUBHA PHABACH **G**
SEANA CHAISTEAL **G**			GREÒTAL **N**
TRÀIGH BAILE FOR THUATH **G**			HOGH BEAG **[N]**
QUINISH **N**			NA SLOCAN DUBHA **G**
BAILENACILLE **G**			SRÒN LITHINIS **[N]**
HALTOSH POINT **[N?]**			SLOC PHABAIGH **G**
TEAMPULL MHÓIRE **G**			SRÒN AN RUBHA **G**
TEAMPULL AN T-SAGAIRT **G**			SRÒN BHEAG AN T-SRUTHA **G**
AN CORRAN **G**			STILL **G/SSE**
TRÀIGH AN T-SEANA-CHAISTEAL **G**			THE BANKS **SSE**
RUBH' AN T-SEANA-CHAISTEIL **G**			TRÀIGH PHABAIGH **G**
RU DUINE **G**			
AM POLL **G**			
LINGAY **N**			
KIRKTOWN **SSE**			
PARK DYKE **SSE**			
TIGH PHLUNKAIT **G**			
TIGH NAM BALACH BEAGA **G**			
THE 'ATH' **G/SSE?**			
TIGH NA SGALAGAN **G**			
BAILE MEADHONACH **G**			
OLD SHEEPWASH **SSE**			

Table 4 Pab(b)ay island names, not including surrounding area names. Names are classified as **G** (Gaelic), **SSE** (Scottish Standard English), **N** (Norse), **[N]** (Norse names incorporated into G or SSE construction), **N?** (probable Norse) and **?** (uncertain).

VIKING-AGE COMMUNITIES

PABBAY (HARRIS) PLACE-NAME INVENTORY

Guide to Entries
Entries formatted for the Scottish Place-Name Database, with the consultation of Simon Taylor, in the following format:

PLACE-NAME *#~[TAB][PARISH] [SITE CLASSIFICATION] [NATIONAL GRID REFERENCE] [CERTAINTY LEVEL 1-5] [ALTITUDE] [ASPECT/DRAINAGE]
   Place-name date reference (i.e. *Place-name* 1865 Otter)

Explanation, derivation and related material[24].

* = not listed on Ordnance Survey Pathfinder
\# = obsolete
~ = linear feature
[PARISH] = 3-letter abbreviation, e.g. HAR for Harris

Site Classification Codes:

A	*Antiquity*
Co	*Coastal*
E	*Ecclesiastical*
F	*Field*
I	*Island*
O	*Other*
R	*Relief*
S	*Settlement*
W	*Water (not Coastal)*

Certainty Level:

1 – certain
2 – assumed
3 – within 1km in each direction
4 – within 5km in each direction
5 – vague (whole island or parish)

Aspect/Drainage = South-West Facing (SWF), West Facing (WEF), ...

---

[24] As outlined earlier, this inventory is primarily a collection of data (with an eye to the older material). Correspondingly, modern Gaelic names are generally not translated in this explanatory entry.

VIKING-AGE COMMUNITIES

Abbreviations (in chronological order)

Lew Har = Anon. c1600-30. [*Lewis and Harris*]. Location: National Library of Ireland MS. 2656. no XXIII.

Atlas Novus = J Blaeu 1654. *Atlas Novus*. Amsterdam.

Martin/map = Martin Martin 1703. *A new map of the Western Isles of Scotland*. In M Martin 1703, *A description of the Western Isles of Scotland*, London.

Tiddeman = Mark Tiddeman 1730. (A map of the West Coast and Western Isles). "To the Honorable Sir Charles Wager this draught of part of the Highlands of Scotland is humbleby presented by his most dutyfull and most obedient humble sarvant Mark Tiddeman 1730." Location: NLS.

Keulen = Gerard van Keulen 1734? *Nieuwe paskaart van de West Kust van Schotland, de Lewys Eylanden en de noord Kust van Yrland*. In I van Keulen 1734, *De Niewe Groote Ligtende Zee-Fakkel*. Location: BM, Bod, NLS, RGS.

Huddart = Joseph Huddart 1794. *A new chart of the West coast of Scotland from the point of Ardnamurchan to Cape Wrath*. In J Huddart 1794, *The North-about Navigator*, London.

Heather/Hebrides = William Heather 1804. "A new and improved chart of the Hebrides or Lewis Islands and adjacent coast of Scotland from the Mull of Cantire to Cape Wrath". Location: BM, NLS.

Bald/Harris = William Bald 1805. "Map of Harris". Repr W Ballantine 1829, [Lithography], Edinburgh. Location: NLS.

Thomson/Western Isles Mid = John Thomson 1822. *Middle part of Western Isles*. In John Thomson 1832, *Atlas of Scotland*, Edinburgh.

Scot W = 1886. *Scotland: West Coast*. [Admiralty Chart no 2635]. Location: NLS.

Otter = H C Otter *et al* 1872. *Hebrides or Western Isles from Barra Head to Scarpa Id*. [Admiralty Chart no 2474]. Location: NLS.

SSS PNS85/2 = School of Scottish Studies PNS85/2. Recorded 8/1985. Informants: Bill Lawson, I.D.P. Stornoway, Kerry Campbell, farm manager for Pabbay, resident Leverburgh, Harris, Neil McDonald, now resident Bearsden, Glasgow, ex-Harris: his grandfather belonged to Pabbay. Accompanying map missing.

MacKillop = Donald MacKillop 1991. *Sea-Names of Berneray Ainmean-Mhara Bhearnaraigh*. Repr of Rocks, Skerries, Shoals and Islands in the Sound of Harris and Uist and around the island of Berneray, *Transactions of the Gaelic Society of Inverness*, vol lvi (1988-90): 428-502.

VIKING-AGE COMMUNITIES

Parish information
"Harris. Harige – Hary – Harrage – Parsonage of Sact Bryde in Harrage – Herreis.

Harris, of old named also the Ardmanach of Lewis, is the southern and more mountainous part of that island, rendered peninsular by Loch Resort on the west and Loch Seaforth on the east, and midway nearly subdivided into two by East and West Loch Tarbert. From its extreme south to the boundary of Lewis there runs an elevated ridge, varying from 2000 to 3000 feet above the sea. The coast is much indented, and around it lie the islands Scarp, Taransay, Pabay, Berneray, Ensay, Killigray, Scalpay, and many of smaller size.

Besides the churches of Saint Bride and Saint Clement there were in Harris and its islands many churches or chapels, the ruins of which existed in 1790. Of these … in Pabbay the churches of Saint Mary and Saint Muluag…

In this parish there are numerous vestiges of its early possession by the Northmen, such as round forts, of which the most remarkable is the fort at Borve or Borough in Harris." (Bannatyne Club, *Origines Parochiales Scotiae* 1854: 376-9)

Place-name inventory
PABBAY ~ HAR I NF894885 1 196m
    Pabpa c.1620-30 Lew Har
    Papa 1654 *Atlas Novus* Æbudæ Insulæ, sive Hebrides/The Westerne Iles of Scotland
    Papa 1654 *Atlas Novus* Leogus et Haraia/Lewis and Haray
    Papa 1654 *Atlas Novus* Uistus Insula
    Pabay 1703 Martin/map
    Papa 1734? Keulen
    Pabbay I. 1794 Huddart [*I.* = Island]
    Pabbay 1804 Heather/Hebrides
    Pabbay 1805 Bald/Harris
    Pabbay 1822 Thomson/Western Isles Mid
    Pabbay 1865 Otter
    Pabbay 1865x1886 Scot W
    Pabbay 1881 OS 6 inch first edn.
    Pabbay 1975 OS Pathf
    Pabaigh 1996 OS Landranger

FORMERLY CALLED *Tarrensey I.* on 1730 Tiddeman (probable confusion of *Pabbay I.* for *Tarrensey I.*). Between NF869879 (W) and NF910876 (E) and NF891893 (N) and NF887864 (S).

"My first job after I left school was in Pabay with the bard Roderick MacDonald and his two brothers, both named Donald. I was there to help them look after the deer and the sheep. It was wartime [presumably WWII] and meat was valuable. Pabay isle was isolated and raiders could quite easily help themselves. We had rifles, guns and ammunition, but to my disappointment all we ever saw was the friendliest faces of fishermen from Berneray and the men with stores from Harris where the owner resided. My experience as a cast-away on this island, which was uninhabited, will have to wait for another time, but it was the most interesting experience, and the most educational, of my whole life." (MacKillop 1991: 43-4)[25]

"Neil Morrison, the Pabay bard, born in Harris in 1816, was a shepherd ... he only lived a few years on the isle of Pabay which he found black and depressing. I personally spent a full term there from October to April [c. WWII] as a boy of 15 years. To me the experience was a very happy one, despite the shortage of company; the total population was only four people, two shepherds, their older brother and myself as assistant. Morrison was well aware of the wild conditions prevailing off the North Uist shore ...

The Song of Fear (Verse 8)
'si mi nach iarradh an sealladh,
A bhi 'g amhrac na cìosanaich, * (overpowering waves)[26]
Stigh bho Haisgeir nan ròn,
A mach bho shorn Rhu Ghriminnis,
'G éisdeachd fuaim Garrai Grànnda,
'Nall ó Bhalai cha bhinn leam e,
'S gob Rhu Rhosagaidh 'm Pabbai,
Far nach stadadh an drìlleachan." (MacKillop 1991: 56)

English translation courtesy of Rachel Craig:

The Song of Fear (Verse 8)
It is I that would not want the view,
Seeing the overpowering waves,
Coming in from Haiskeir Island [NF61 82] of the seals,
Out from the point of Griminish Point [NF72 76],
Hearing the sound of Gearraidh Grànnda [grim wall?],
Over from Vallay [NF78 76], that is not a sweet sound for me,
And the point of Rosikie Point [NF89 88] in Pabbay,
Where the oyster-catcher would not rest.

ALARIP BAY ~   HAR Co NF884891 1 0m NWF
    Alarip Bay 1881 OS 6 inch first edn.
    Alarip Bay 1975 OS Pathf
    Bagh Alairip 1996 OS Landranger

FORMERLY CALLED *Linen Cove*. Reference point taken from middle of bay. ON *áll* + ON *hóp* 'bay', where *áll*, m, may carry the meaning 'eel' or alternatively 'deep, narrow channel' or possibly 'deep valley' (cf *Ålborg* in Denmark).

---

[25] The purpose of this catalogue is to present all relevant data (preserving original form and content, i.e. neither spellings nor interpretations have been corrected – but have sometimes been commented upon). In cases where other work informs material thus presented, this too has been incorporated. The resulting collected materials thus form a resource for further scholarship beyond the scope of work undertaken here.
[26] Perhaps this word is related to the *Kishinish* name (given below)?

LINEN COVE *#~   HAR Co NF8889 1 0m NWF
  Linen Cove 1805 Bald/Harris

NOW CALLED Alarip Bay.

SCARASDALE POINT   HAR Co NF887893 1 8m NWF
  Ru Scarrisdale 1805 Bald/Harris
  Scarasdale Point 1881 OS 6 inch first edn.
  Scarasdale Point 1975 OS Pathf
  Rubha Scarasdail 1996 OS Landranger

ON *skarð*, n, 'score, notch, open space after something taken out, hole, opening' or *skør* (see below). The -a- in *Scarasdale* is probably a later addition in Gaelic in order to avoid a lengthy consonant cluster. The following entry for *Scurrival* from Stahl's Barra inventory may inform interpretation of the *Scarasdale* name:
  Scurrival *hill of ?*
  Borgstrøm derives this name from the ON Skagag-rif-fjall (Borgstrøm, 1937: 292), 'hill near the reef of the promontory'. According to him the name may have undergone strong contraction. A descriptive name for this important shipping mark appears logical. However, there is the ON name Skorri, which in its genitive case becomes Skorra resulting in the possible translation 'Skorri's hill'. A third interpretation hints at a link with ON skør, f, 'cleft', of which ON skora is the genitive pl., which would translate as 'hill of the clefts', which, too, would make sense in this context. (See Eysteinsson 1992: 14) (Stahl 1999: 255)

BREMISH POINT   HAR Co NF902893 1 8m NOF
  Ru Branish 1865 Otter
  Bremish Point 1881 OS 6 inch first edn.
  Bremish Point 1975 OS Pathf
  Rubha Bhreinis 1996 OS Landranger

ON *breið nis* 'broad ness'.

TARRENSEY I. *#~ HAR I NF8988 1
  Tarrensey I. 1730 Tiddeman [*I.* = Island]

NOW CALLED *Pabbay*. Probable confusion of *Tarrensey I.* for *Pabbay I.*

KISHINISH   HAR RCo NF876889 1 30m NWF
  Ru Histinish 1805 Bald/Harris
  Ru Kishinish 1865 Otter
  Kishinish 1881 OS 6 inch first edn.
  Kishinish 1975 OS Pathf
  Cisinis 1996 OS Landranger

ON ? *kjós* 'small bay' + ON *nes*. Stahl (1999: 214) derives *Kisimul*, in the Barra group, as 'rock of the small bay'. If her derivation can be extended to *Kishinish*, then it would signify 'peninsula of the small bay'. Stahl gives the following discussion of *Kisimul*:

> The specific is unlikely to derive from the ON personal name Kisi which Lind (1915) classifies as a manipulated medieval name. Allan McDonald (1903) provides the essential clue by giving Ciasmul as an alternative spelling which leads to the derivation from ON kjóss, m, 'small bay' and ON múli, m, 'headland', here 'sea-rock'. Kisimul provides an accurate geographic setting for this derivation. (Stahl 1999: 214)

A problem, however, with linking *Kisimul* to *Kishinish* is that the 's' of the first element is not palatalised, whereas the 's' of *Kishinish* clearly is.

Alternatively, *Kishinish* (or *Kis(h)imul*) could be related to the word *cìosanaich*, used in Neil Morrison's *The Song of Fear* (under the PABBAY name entry above).

MEAHALL ~ HAR R NF879882 1 76m
    Meaulle 1805 Bald/Harris
    Meahall 1881 OS 6 inch first edn.
    Meahall 1975 OS Pathf
    Meahall 1996 OS Landranger

The name of a hill. ON *mjófjall* 'narrow hill'.

MOL A' MHAIDE MHÓIR   HAR Co NF874886 1 0m WEF
    Mol a' Mhaide Mhòir 1881 OS 6 inch first edn.
    Mol a' Mhaide Mhóir 1975 OS Pathf
    Mol a' Mhaide Mhóir 1996 OS Landranger

ROSIKIE POINT   HAR Co NF871884 1 0m NWF
    Ru Rosikie 1865 Otter
    Rosikie Point 1881 OS 6 inch first edn.
    Rosikie Point 1975 OS Pathf
    Rubha Rosagaidh 1996 OS Landranger

May contain ON *hross* 'horse' or Gaelic/Pictish *ros* 'promontory'. If this latter word is contained, then it must belong to an older stratum than many of the other Gaelic place-names on the island, since the explanatory element *rubha* 'promontory, point' has been added – resulting in the modern *Rubha Rosagaidh*. Compare to *Rosinish*, 'horse-headland', on the *Pabbay* near Barra:

> A combination of ON hross, n, 'horse' and ON nes, n, 'headland'. (Stahl 1999: 245-6)

MacKillop (1991: 56) supplies the earliest name form *Rhu Rhosagaidh* when he quotes Neil Morrison's poem. Neil Morrison was born in 1816; thus we can imagine an early to mid nineteenth-century date for his poem. It is not known, however, if MacKillop modernised the spelling of place-names in this poem. From other forms he supplies, such as *Rhu Ghriminnis*, it appears he did not modernise the Gaelic. If this is the case, then *Rhu Rhosagaidh* is an important early form.

VOLRI GEO   HAR RCo NF873883 1 8m NWF
    Volri Geo 1881 OS 6 inch first edn.
    Volri Geo 1975 OS Pathf

Probable Norse name.

GREANAN   HAR R NF885887 1 114m WEF
    Grinance 1805 Bald/Harris
    Greanan 1881 OS 6 inch first edn.
    Greanan 1975 OS Pathf
    Greanan 1996 OS Landranger

West facing slope of hill. Compare to *Grianan* (Stahl 1999: 208) and *Grean* (Stahl 1999: 207), which, may be derived either from Gaelic *grian*, 'sun', meaning 'sunny spot', or from the ON adj. *grœn*, 'green', meaning 'green spot'. That the OS Landranger 18 (1996), which gaelicises all names, has *Greanan*, suggests that whoever was their local informant did not consider that this name had anything to do with Gaelic *grian* 'sun'. This observation then points to an Old Norse derivation. The ending may, however, be Gaelic.

LOCH HEDDAL BEG   HAR W NF884881 1 46m SWF
    Loch Heddal Beg 1881 OS 6 inch first edn.
    Loch Heddal Beg 1975 OS Pathf

Name contains *Loch Heddal*.

LOCH HEDDAL MORE   HAR W NF883883 1 46m SOF
    Loch Heddaule 1805 Bald/Harris
    L. Hesiel 1865 Otter
    Loch Heddal More 1881 OS 6 inch first edn.
    Loch Heddal More 1975 OS Pathf
    Loch Sheudail Mor 1996 OS Landranger

FORMERLY CALLED *Lingay* (probable misunderstanding of source for *Lingay Burn*). Name contains *Loch Heddal*.

LOCH HEDDAL *   HAR W NF88 88 1

Name is part of *Loch Heddal More* and *Loch Heddal Beg*, and contains *Heddal* (Sheudail), q.v.

HEDDAL *   HAR R NF88 88 2

This place-name survives only in the loch-names *Loch Heddal More* and *Loch Heddal Beg*. Its Gaelic form is given on OS Landranger 18 (1996) as *Loch Sheudail* (Mor). The

-dd- of *Loch Heddal* suggests a short preceding vowel, but the *Loch Sheudail* form gives a long e. It is probably an ON name containing *dalr* 'valley'. The first element (the specific) may be ON *há* 'high', together giving ? *há(r) dal(r)* 'high valley'. Another, perhaps more probable, proposal would derive the specific from ON *heiðr* 'moor, heath' or *hey* 'hay' (cf *Heddle* in Firth in Orkney).

LINGAY *#   HAR W NF881881 1
    Lingay 1822 Thomson/Western Isles Mid

NOW CALLED *Loch Heddal More* and *Loch Heddal Beg* (probable misunderstanding of the source for *Lingay Burn*). ON *ling* 'heather' + *á* 'river, burn'.

BEINN A' CHARNAIN   HAR R NF894885 1 196m
    Ben na Harnine 1805 Bald/Harris
    Pk. of Pabbay 1865 Otter [*Pk.* = Peak]
    Beinn a' Chárnain 1881 OS 6 inch first edn.
    Beinn a' Charnain 1975 OS Pathf
    Beinn a' Charnain 1996 OS Landranger

BAILE-FO-THUATH   HAR S NF904882 1 53m EAF
    Baile-fo-thuath 1881 OS 6 inch first edn.
    Baile-fo-thuath 1975 OS Pathf

LOCH NA H-EASGAINN   HAR W Co NF873874 1 0m
    Loch na h-Easgainn 1881 OS 6 inch first edn.
    Loch na h-Easgainn 1975 OS Pathf
    Loch na h-Easgainn 1996 OS Landranger

'Loch of the eel' (Gaelic *easgann*, gen. *easgainne* f. 'eel').

OSE   HAR F NF874876 1 8m WEF
    Ose 1881 OS 6 inch first edn.
    Ose 1975 OS Pathf
    Os 1996 OS Landranger

ON *óss* 'river- or burn-mouth'.

OSE POINT   HAR Co NF870874 1 0m WEF
    Ru Oze 1805 Bald/Harris
    Ose Point 1881 OS 6 inch first edn.
    Ose Point 1975 OS Pathf
    Rubha Os 1996 OS Landranger

FORMERLY CALLED *Broad Rks*.

BROAD RKS *#   HAR Co NF870874 1 0m WEF

Broad Rks. 1865 Otter [*Rks.* = Rocks]

NOW CALLED *Ose Point*. This is possibly a description, rather than a name.

CREAG HURISTEN HAR R NF888876 1 61m
    Creag Huristen 1881 OS 6 inch first edn.
    Creag Huristen 1975 OS Pathf
    Creag Hurasden 1985 SSS PNS85/2
    Creag Thuristein 1996 OS Landranger

According to SSS PNS85/2, "with cave underneath". Perhaps a Gaelic name which contains a male personal name deriving from ON *Þórsteinn*. Thus 'Thorstein's Rock or Crag' – perhaps related to lost folklore?

TEAMPULL BEAG HAR EA NF889872 1 23m SOF
    Teampull Beag 1881 OS 6 inch first edn.
    Teampull Beag 1975 OS Pathf

Gaelic 'little church'.

TOTA REBEIN HAR R NF881872 1 30m
    Tota Rebein 1881 OS 6 inch first edn.
    Tota Rebein 1975 OS Pathf
    Tobhta Reabain 1996 OS Landranger

Containing the Norse loan-word *topt* 'toft, homestead, site of a building', which in Gaelic developed the secondary meaning 'ruin' (Gammeltoft 2001). *Rebein* may contain a Norse-derived personal name (or may derive from Biblical Reuben).

BAILE-LINGAY HAR S NF894875 1 40m SOF
    Lingay 1805 Bald/Harris
    Baile-lingay 1881 OS 6 inch first edn.
    Baile-lingay 1975 OS Pathf

Mid-point of settlement given; settlement stretches between NF894873 (S) and NF894877 (N). According to SSS PNS85/2 (1985), both the original farm of *Baile Lingay* and the larger crofts were cleared in 1842. This source also notes upper crofts belonging to *Baile Lingay* and the place-name *Tigh na Sgalagan*, where the farmhouses for the original farm of *Baile Lingay* lived.

NA MULLAICHEAN HAR R NF899879 1 99m SEF
    Na Mullaichean 1881 OS 6 inch first edn.
    Na Mullaichean 1975 OS Pathf
    Na Mullaichean 1996 OS Landranger

'The hills, tops', plural of Gaelic *mullach* (m). OS Object Name Books (Bk 5 Rl 107 Pg 139) describes this as "a small ridge covered with good rough pasture".

LINGAY BURN ~   HAR W NF898867 1 0m SEF
    Lingay Burn 1881 OS 6 inch first edn.
    Lingay Burn 1975 OS Pathf

ON *Lingá (ON *ling* 'heather' + *á* 'river, burn') + Scots *burn*.

RUBH' A' BHAILE FO THUATH   HAR RCo NF908879 1 23m EAF
    Rubh' a' Bhaile Fo Thuath 1881 OS 6 inch first edn.
    Rubh' a' Bhaile Fo Thuath 1975 OS Pathf
    Rubh' a' Bhaile Fo Thuath 1996 OS Landranger

FORMERLY CALLED *Reef* and *Ginnoch*.

REEF *#   HAR RCo NF908879 1 23m EAF
    Reef Point 1794 Huddart
    Reef Point 1804 Heather/Hebrides
    Reef Point 1805 Bald/Harris
    The Reef 1865 Otter

NOW CALLED *Rubh' a' Bhaile Fo Thuath*.

GINNOCH *#   HAR RCo NF908879 1 23m EAF
    Ginnoch 1822 Thomson/Western Isles Mid

NOW CALLED *Rubh' a' Bhaile Fo Thuath*.

SEANA CHAISTEAL   HAR S NF902872 1 23m SEF
    Duine 1805 Bald/Harris
    [unreadable] 1865 Otter
    Seana Chaisteal 1881 OS 6 inch first edn.
    Seana Chaisteal 1975 OS Pathf
    Seana Chaisteal 1996 OS Landranger

Gaelic *sean* + Gaelic *caisteal*, 'old castle'. OS Object Name Books (Bk 5 Rl 107 Pg 141) describes *Seana Chaisteal* and *Site of Dùn* as two separate places, noting the *Dùn* lies "17 chains west from the ruins of the ancient chapels on the island of Pabbay" (see Sheet 21 Trace 5), whereas *Seana Chaisteal* is situated "at the east side of the island of Pabbay" (Bk 5 Rl 107 Pg 140).

TRÁIGH BAILE FOR THUATH ~   HAR Co NF906874 1 0m SEF
    Tráigh Baile Fo Thuath 1881 OS 6 inch first edn.
    Tráigh Baile Fo Thuath 1975 OS Pathf
    Tràigh Baile Fo Thuath 1996 OS Landranger

Beach stretches between NF904870 (SW) and NF908876 (NE).

QUINISH   HAR Co NF878863 1 0m SWF
    Ru Quinish 1805 Bald/Harris
    Ru Quinish 1881 OS 6 inch first edn.
    Quinish 1975 OS Pathf
    Cuidhnis 1996 OS Landranger

ON *kví* 'cattle or sheep fold' + *nes*. Peninsula connected to *Pabbay* on 1881 OS 6 inch first edn. It now seems to refer to a group of small islands or rocks off the south-west coast of *Pabbay*. Note the addition of *rubha* in the earliest forms.

BAILENACILLE   HAR S NF887867 1 15m SEF
    Balinkily 1794 Huddart
    Balinkily 1804 Heather/Hebrides
    Kirktown 1805 Bald/Harris
    Kirktown 1822 Thomson/Western Isles Mid
    Bailenacille 1881 OS 6 inch first edn.
    Bailenacille 1975 OS Pathf
    Bailenacille 1996 OS Landranger

G *baile* + G *an* + G *cill*. 'Kirkton or farm or village of the church'. The church in question is *Teampull Mhóire*. According to SSS PNS85/2, part of the *Baile na Cille* was demolished for stones to build the *Park Dyke*; the whole of *Baile na Cille* was cleared in 1846.

HALTOSH POINT   HAR Co NF887864 1 0m SOF
    Haltosh Point 1881 OS 6 inch first edn.
    Haltosh Point 1975 OS Pathf
    Rubha Thaltois 1996 OS Landranger

Probable Norse name with unclear generic.

TEAMPULL MHÓIRE   HAR EA NF889869 1 8m SEF
    Ch. 1865 Otter
    Teampull Mhóire 1881 OS 6 inch first edn.
    Teampull Mhóire 1975 OS Pathf
    Teampall Mhóire 1996 Os Landranger

SAME AS *Teampull an t-Sagairt*. 'Mary's Church'. Accompanying Sheepfold and Graveyard listed on 1881 OS 6 inch first edn. Otter (1865) notes a *Ch.* [church] here.

TEAMPULL AN T-SAGAIRT *   HAR EA NF889869 1 8m SEF
    Teampull an t-Sagairt 1985 SSS PNS85/2

VIKING-AGE COMMUNITIES

SAME AS *Teampull Mhòire*.

AN CORRAN HAR Co NF896864 1 0m SEF
  Corran Point 1805 Bald/Harris
  Corran Pt. 1865 Otter [*Pt.* = Point]
  An Corran 1881 OS 6 inch first edn.
  An Corran 1975 OS Pathf
  An Corran 1996 OS Landranger

TRÀIGH AN T-SEANA-CHAISTEAL ~ HAR Co NF899867 1 0m SEF
  Tràigh an t-Seana-chaisteal 1881 OS 6 inch first edn.
  Tràigh an t-Seana-chaisteal 1975 OS Pathf
  Tràigh an t-Seana-chaisteal 1996 OS Landranger

RUBH' AN T-SEANA-CHAISTEIL ~ HAR Co NF904870 1 0m SEF
  Rudh' an t-Seana-chaisteil 1881 OS 6 inch first edn.
  Rubh' an t-Seana-chaisteil 1975 OS Pathf
  Rubh' an t-Seana-chaisteil 1996 OS Landranger

FORMERLY CALLED *Ru Duine*.

RU DUINE *#~ HAR Co NF904870 1 0m SEF

  Ru Duine 1805 Bald/Harris
  Ru Dune 1865 Otter

NOW CALLED *Rubh' an t-Seana-Chaisteil*.

AM POLL *# HAR Co NF889865 2 0m
  Am Poll OS Object Name Books (Bk 5 Rl 107 Pg 135)

Noted as *Landing Place* on 1805 Bald/Harris, 1822 Thomson/Western Isles Mid, OS Object Name Books (Bk 5 Rl 107 Pg 135), and 1881 OS 6 inch first edn.

LINGAY *#~ HAR S NF8988 3
  Lingay 1805 Bald/Harris

ON *ling* 'heather' + *á* 'river, burn'. On Bald's map of 1805, *Pabbay* divided into two parts: *Lingay* and *Kirktown*. Note that *Lingay* appears on Thomson/Western Isles Mid (1822) as a name for *Loch Heddal More* and *Loch Heddal Beg* (a probable misunderstanding of the source for *Lingay Burn*).

KIRKTOWN *#~ HAR S NF8887 3
  Kirktown 1805 Bald/Harris

On Bald's map of 1805, *Pabbay* divided into two parts: *Lingay* and *Kirktown*.

PARK DYKE *   HAR O NF89 88 5
    Park Dyke 1985 SSS PNS85/2

Built after the island was cleared.

TIGH PHLUNKAIT *   HAR S NF89 88 5
    Tigh Phlunkait 1985 SSS PNS85/2

After Mr Plunkett, current owner of *Pabbay*. Built circa May 1985, imported from Norway.

TIGH NAM BALACH BEAGA *   HAR S NF89 88 5
    Tigh nam Balach Beaga 1985 SSS PNS85/2

The only house left habitable after 1846.

THE 'ATH' * HAR S NF89 87 2
    The 'Ath' 1985 SSS PNS85/2

The 'Ath' of *Creag Huristen*, cleared 1846.

TIGH NA SGALAGAN *   HAR S NF89 87 5
    Tigh na Sgalagan 1985 SSS PNS85/2

Where the farmworkers for the original farm of *Baile Lingay* lived.

BAILE MEADHONACH *   HAR S NF89 87 5
    Baile Meadhonach 1985 SSS PNS85/2

Covered by sand dunes.

OLD SHEEPWASH *   HAR S NF89 87 5
    Old Sheepwash 1985 SSS PNS85/2

Surrounding sea and island names
PABBAY I. *#~   HAR I NB0301 1
    Pabbay I. 1730 Tiddeman

NOW CALLED *Taransay*. Probable confusion of *Pabbay I.* for *Tarrensey I.*

SHILLAY ~   HAR I NF878914 1 79m
    Soa Moir 1654 *Atlas Novus* Leogus et Haraia/Lewis and Haray
    Soa Moir 1654 *Atlas Novus* Uistus Insula
    Shillay I. 1794 Huddart

Shillay Isle 1804 Heather/Hebrides
Shillay Island 1805 Bald/Harris
Schillay I. 1822 Thomson/Western Isles Mid
Schillay 1865 Otter
Shillay 1865x1886 Scot W
Shillay 1881 OS 6 inch first edn.
Shillay 1975 OS Pathf
Siolaigh 1996 OS Landranger

MacKillop postulates that this name derives from ON *selr* 'seal':

> People were never living on Shillay, but its name in O.N. means Seal Island. There is a large healthy colony of seals on the island till this day and it must have survived from the time of the Vikings, who give it the name it still has today. (MacKillop 1991: 56)

However, the *soa*-element in the two oldest source forms of *Soa Moir* instead appear to derive from ON **Sauðey* 'sheep island'. Though possible, two name forms for that island would be surprising.

AIRD AN LAOIGH   HAR Co NF877907 1 8m SOF
Ru Airdna Leugh 1805 Bald/Harris
Ard an Laoigh 1881 OS 6 inch edn.
Aird an Laoigh 1975 OS Pathf
Aird an Laoigh 1996 OS Landranger

LITTLE SHILLAY   HAR I NF874906 1 30m
Soa beg 1654 *Atlas Novus* Leogus et Haraia/Lewis and Haray
Soa beg 1654 *Atlas Novus* Uistus Insula
Little Shillay 1805 Bald/Harris
Little Shillay 1822 Thomson/Western Isles Mid
Little Shillay 1865 Otter
Little Shillay 1881 OS 6 inch first edn.
Little Shillay 1975 OS Pathf
Siolaigh Bheag 1996 OS Landranger

SOUND OF SPUIR ~ HAR Co NF8685 1
Sound of Sporr 1865 Otter
Sound of Spoor 1881 OS 6 inch first edn.
Sound of Spuir 1975 OS Pathf
Caolas Spuir 1996 OS Landranger

SPUIR   NUS I NF853843 1 8m
Spor 1654 *Atlas Novus* Uistus Insulus
Spur 1805 Bald/Harris
Sporr 1865 Otter
Sporr 1865x1886 Scot W
Spoor 1881 OS 6 inch first edn.

Spuir 1975 OS Pathf
Spuir 1996 OS Landranger

FORMERLY CALLED *Fure Isle*. MacKillop proposes the following:
> Spuir – W. of Berneray, between the island of Boreray and the isle of Pabay. This is the name given to a tiny but fairly high island. Spuir or Spor is spur, claw or talon. Norse, spori, a spur. The name is likely to mean claw or talon. (MacKillop 1991: 37)

However, this name could formally be a Gaelic name, cf Gaelic *spuir* 'spur, talon'. An alternative ON origin could be ON *sporðr*, m, 'spur, end, tail (on fish, snakes, etc)'.

FURE ISLE *#   NUS I NF853843 2
Fure Isle 1804 Heather/Hebrides

NOW CALLED *Spuir*.

SKYR NARNON *# NUS I NF8585 4
Skyr 1654 *Atlas Novus* Leogus et Haraia/Lewis and Haray
Skyr narnon 1654 *Atlas Novus* Uistus Insula

SPOR REEF *HAR Co NF8685 3
Spor Reef 1865 Otter

NE of Spuir.

SOUND OF PABBAY ~   HAR Co NF9084 1
Sound of Pabbay 1865 Otter
Sound of Pabbay 1881 OS 6 inch first edn.
Sound of Pabbay 1975 OS Pathf
Caolas Phabaigh 1996 OS Landranger

SOUND OF SHILLAY ~   HAR Co NF885898 1
Sound of Shillay 1865 Otter
Sound of Shillay 1865x1886 Scot W
Sound of Shillay 1881 OS 6 inch first edn.
Sound of Shillay 1975 OS Pathf
Caolas Siolaigh 1996 OS Landranger

OITIR AN T-SEANN CHAISTEIL *   HAR Co NF9286 4
Oitir an t-Seann Chaisteil 1991 MacKillop

"Oitir an t-Seann Chaisteil – Off the Pabay shore near a point where there was a castle at one time. Oitir, shoal; sean, old, and the last word is G. for castle. Translates to, Sand bank of the Old Castle. The MacLeods had a castle in Pabay isle at one time." (MacKillop 1991: 47)

VIKING-AGE COMMUNITIES

BODHA ALAIG BHIG *   HAR Co NF8890 3
  Bodha Alaig Bhig 1991 MacKillop

The Scottish Gaelic (ScG) *bodha* 'hidden reef' is itself a borrowing from ON *boði*.
"Bodha Alaig Bhig – N. of Pabay, bet. it and the isle of Shillay. Alaig is for Alexander. Bhig is from G. beag, small. Searock of Alexander Beag. This was a MacDonald from Berneray. His progenitors came from Pabay. This was to differentiate from his brother, also named Alexander, but locally known as Big Alex. These brothers, along with a crewman, Norman Paterson, were lobster fishing near this rock when a large breaker smashed over the boat, sweeping away the mast and sail, and only the expert seamanship of the crew stopped the boat from being engulfed. They managed to hold on to the oars and rowed the boat to calmer waters on the south side of the island, where the Pabay shepherds, the MacDonald brothers, rendered assistance and helped them to retrieve the mast and sail which was washed ashore on the northern side of the island. Big Alexander's grandsons are today following the same trade." (MacKillop 1991: 47-8)

BODHA LEITHEACH CAOLAIS * HAR Co NF9085 3
  Bodha Leitheach Caolais 1991 MacKillop

"Bodha Leitheach Caolais – Half-Way bet. An Corran of Pabay and Carragh Léithe, Berneray; given on charts as, *Bo Leac Caolas*. This is an absurdity. The Admiralty did indeed wonderful work in surveying the Hebrides, only to have it marred by very odd Gaelic spelling, considering the number of high ranking, Gaelic speaking officers in the Royal and Merchant Navy who were available to them. Leitheach is half-way. Caolais is from Caol, kyle. Half-way searock of the Kyle. The word léithe, is greyness, comp. of liath. The old people referred to this carragh or rock in the manner given." (MacKillop 1991: 48)

FIREAN LEITHEACH CAOLAIS * HAR Co NF8885 3
  Firean Leitheach Caolais 1991 MacKillop

"Firean Churabhrat – Rocks off the S. of Pabay isle. The meaning of this name is not clear, cf., *Na Fireanan*, also off Pabay, on the East side." (MacKillop 1991: 48)

NA FIREANAN *   HAR Co NF9287 3
  Na Fireanan 1991 MacKillop

"Na Fireanan – These sea rocks are E. of the former township of Baile Fo Thuath, in the Isle of Pabay. Translated on charts as, Halo Rock. The relationship between the names is vague and should really read, The Truthful Ones. These rocks are visible from the little clachan of Brusda, in Berneray, the residents of which could foretell coming storms by turbulence in the sea causing foaming breakers to crash over the rocks and up into the air. Forecasting the weather by means of these rocks was so accurate that they have been known ever since as the truthful ones. Donald, son of John Morrison, when resident in Brudawas asked to judge the weather and he replied in his usual enigmatic matter, as follows, 'the Truthful Ones are going up in the skies, but the Wicked One is not moving.' 'Tha Na Fireanan a' dol dhan athar ach chan eil an t-Aingidh a' gluasad.' …" (MacKillop 1991: 24-5)

GRUAGACH *   HAR Co NF9386 4
    A' Gruagach 1991 MacKillop

Skerry.

"A' Gruagach – This is a low-lying skerry in the triangle of the sea, formed between the islands of Berneray, Pabay and Killigray. The Maiden, is a literal translation of the name. This name can also mean in Gaelic, a brownie or a sprite; perhaps in this case a sea-sprite. As far as I know, there is no extant tradition concerning this rock in the sea." (MacKillop 1991: 25)

BODHA NÈILL *   HAR Co NF853845 2
    Bodha Nèill 1991 MacKillop

"Bodha Nèill – N. of Spuir, about two hundred yards or so from the islet. Bodha, a rock over which the waves break; Nèill gen. case of Nìall the G. for Neil. Believed to be Neil MacKillop, a lobster fisherman, mentioned previously. This Neil was my grandfather. Sea-rock of Neil." (MacKillop 1991: 38)

BODHA SHEONAIDH CHOINNICH *   HAR Co NF8784 3
    Bodha Sheonaidh Choinnich 1991 MacKillop

"Bodha Sheonaidh Choinnich – N.E. of Iver Rocks. In G. Seonaidh is John and Coinneach is Kenneth (this was John MacAskill). Sea-rock of John son of Kenneth, John was a lobster fisherman from Berneray. Both names (masc. nouns) are aspirated." (MacKillop 1991: 38)

SGEIREAN IOMHAIR *~   HAR Co NF870835 2
    Sgeirean Iomhair 1991 MacKillop

The ScG name *Iomhar* derives from On *Ivarr*.
"Sgeirean Iomhair – Eastward from the N. tip of Boreray Isle, a fair distance out on the way to the isle of Pabay. Skerries of Ivor. Given on charts as McIver rocks. In former days a trading smack from the isle of Lewis was sailing southwards with a cargo of salt fish and apparently this Ivor McIver struck his boat on a skerry here. In this area a sure way of having a skerry called after you. McIver's destination was Liverpool, a long haul in a small sailing craft. N.B. This MacIver from Carloway in Lewis is said to be one of the MacIvers who set up the famous Cunard line." (MacKillop 1991: 38)

BODHA MÓR CHNOC NAN CLAIGEANN *   HAR Co NF9185 4
    Bodha Mor Chnoc nan Claigeann 1991 MacKillop

"Bodha Mór, Bodha Beag and Chnoc nan Claigeann – are further out in the sea between Berneray and Pabay isles. Cnoc is G. for a hillock, and nan Claigeann is Gen. case of Skulls, Knoll of Skulls. This first part of the name translates to the Large and the Small Sea rock. The full name translates to the Large and the Small Sea rock of the Knoll of the Skulls. The reason for this unusual name is because of a sea-bearing; keeping *One Mile Skerry* in line with *The Knoll of Skulls* guides a boat directly to these sea rocks which were popular for lobster fishing. ... Cnoc nan Claigeann is a knoll in the Siabaigh area of Berneray." (MacKillop 1991: 39)

BODHA BEAG CHNOC NAN CLAIGEANN *   HAR Co NF9185 4
Bodha Beag Chnoc nan Claigeann 1991 MacKillop

See *Bodha Mor Chnoc nan Claigeann*.

OITIR NAN CAPULL *   HAR Co NF8984 4
Oitir nan Capull 1991 MacKillop

"Oitir nan Capull – N.E. of Searock Vessel, between Berneray and Pabay. Oitir is a ridge or bank in the sea. Capull is usually a name for a horse or mare and sometimes a bird or another animal. There may be a marine species, unidentified in this case. This sandbank used to be good for fishing flounders, etc. Sadly most of these banks today yield nothing." (MacKillop 1991: 41)

Selected[27] names from the region
SEÒLAID NAM PABACH *~   HAR Co NF978822-NF998795 2
Seòlaid nam Pabach 1991 MacKillop

"Seòlaid nam Pabach – E. from the Kylie group. Seòlaid, fairway; nam Pabach, of the Pabay people. Fairway of the Pabay Men. This channel runs N.E. from Kylie past the long skerries consisting of Langa Sk., Thackdla Sk. and Hard Sk. Keeping the Hard Skerry to the S., this leads to the Isle of Grothaigh (Groay on charts) which belongs to Harris and where the Pabay men cut peats as the supply of their own island was exhausted. The following lines were given to me as a facetious example of Pabay English. The only thing it proves is that there was an Isabella residing in Pabay at one time:
    You go to Groay to day, weather very good,
    You go, I go, Iseabel mo phuithar go?
The name Groay is from O.N. grodhr: gróa, to grow; ay is island. Grow Island, or the Growing Island. Perhaps a good source of food, Kylie is from the word Skeiladh?" (MacKillop 1991: 49)

BORERAY ~ NUS I NF849817 1 56m

---

[27] For all *Pab(b)ay* islands, 'selected' names were included if they had ecclesiastical or Norse associations.

Boreray 1654 *Atlas Novus* Uistus Insula
Boreray 1881 OS 6 inch first edn.
Boreray 1975 OS Pathf
Boraraigh 1996 OS Landranger

Derives from ON *borg*, f, 'fortified place' (Stahl 1999: 155).

BERNERAY ~   HAR I NF928834 1 93m
Bernera 1654 *Atlas Novus* Æbudæ Insulæ, sive Hebrides/The Westerne Iles of Scotland
Bernera 1654 *Atlas Novus* Uistus Insula
Berneray 1881 OS 6 inch first edn.
Berneray 1975 OS Pathf
Bearnaraigh 1996 OS Landranger

Stahl writes of *Berneray*, near Barra:
> Borgstrøm discusses this name in Campbell, 1936: 289. He suggests Bearnaraidh as G spelling and Bjarnarey as ON spelling. The specific is derived from ON bjørn, m, 'bear' or from the ON personal name Bjørn [*biarnar / Biarnar*, gen sg of *björn* 'bear' / *Björn*]. The generic is derived from ON ey, f, 'island'. (Stahl 1999: 146)

KILLEGRAY ~   HAR I NF973840 1 38m
Kellgyr 1654 *Atlas Novus* Uistus Insula
Killegray 1881 OS 6 inch first edn.
Killegray 1975 OS Pathf
Ceileagraigh 1996 OS Landranger

MacKillop proposes the following:
> Killigray – Kjallard is Norse, and gra, grey. Kjallard; burial place. Burial Place Island. With the Isle of Ensay, these are the largest islands in the sound of Harris, between Berneray and Leverburgh. Both very fertile. (MacKillop 1991: 26)

However, this is unlikely as ON *kjallard* does not exist, let alone mean 'burial ground'. Instead ON **Kerlingarey* is possible, the specific being gen sg of *kerling*, f, 'woman, hag' (cf *Kjeringøy* < *Kellingarøy*, *Norsk Stadnamnleksikon* 1997: 255).

ENSAY ~   HAR I NF978858 1 49m
Enisay 1654 *Atlas Novus* Uistus Insula
Ensay 1881 OS 6 inch first edn.
Ensay 1975 OS Pathf
Easaigh 1996 OS Landranger

MacKillop proposes the following:
> Ensay Isle – Gaelic – Easaigh. From Norse, aer, ewes, and ay, island. Ewe island. (MacKillop 1991: 26)

However, this is unlikely. Instead, this name may derive from ON *Einarsey* 'Einar's island' (cf *Ensjø* < *Einarshaugi*, *Norsk Stadnamnsleksikon* 1997: 136).

HAISKEIR EAGACH ~   NUS I NF598810 1 28m
    Helskyr Egach 1654 *Altas Novus* Æbudæ Insulæ, sive Hebrides/The Westerne Iles of Scotland
    Helskyr Egach 1654 *Atlas Novus* Uistus Insula
    Haskeir Eagach 1878x1880 OS 6 inch first edn.
    Haskeir Eagach 1973 OS Pathf
    Hasgeir Eagach 1996 OS Landranger

See *Haiskeir Island*.

HAISKEIR ISLAND ~   NUS I NF613821 1 39m
    Havelskyr na Meul 1654 *Atlas Novus* Æbudæ Insulæ, sive Hebrides/The Westerne Iles of Scotland
    Hayelskyr na Meul 1654 *Atlas Novus* Uistus Insula
    Haskeir Island 1878x1880 OS 6 inch first edn.
    Haiskeir Island 1973 OS Pathf
    Eilean Hasgeir 1996 OS Landranger

Haiskeir is probably derived from ON *hella*, f, 'flagstone', and ON *sker*, n, 'skerry'.
"I was once told a story about my own grandfather, Neil MacKillop, who decided to spend a week fishing at a rocky isle called Haisgeir. The nearest point of land to this isle is Griminis in North Uist. It lies about 8 miles out in the Atlantic ocean. On a Monday, accompanied by another boat, called the 'Sula' which was skippered by its owner, Donald, son of Calum MacLeod, they set off to Shillay Isle to uplift lobster pots. They lifted their pots and set sail for Haisgeir Isle. Unfortunately the wind dropped and a heavy mist came down on them and the two boats lost sight of each other. My grandfather consulted his 'Crown watch' and told his crew to commence rowing. In those days a crown watch was so called because it cost a crown coin, valued at five shillings. This was the only watch and navigational aid on board. The old man steered the boat till he heard, after a long time, the noise of a current, known as Bun an t-sruthain, off the Uist coast. He then altered course for Haisgeir Isles. After what seemed to be an interminable period of time the old man told my father to keep a look-out from the bows in case they would strike Haisgeir suddenly in the mist and damage the boat... [continues to page 10]" (MacKillop 1991: 3-10)

HEISKER ~   NUS I NF616625 1 19m
    Helskyr na Monich 1654 *Atlas Novus* Æbudæ Insulæ, sive Hebrides/The Westerne Iles of Scotland
    Helskyr na Monich 1654 *Atlas Novus* Uistus Insula
    Heisker 1973 OS Pathf
    Theisgeir 1996 OS Landranger

ALSO CALLED *Monach Islands*. See *Monach Islands*.

MONACH ISLANDS ~   NUS I NF616625 1 19m
    Helskyr na Monich 1654 *Atlas Novus* Æbudæ Insulæ, sive Hebrides/The Westerne Iles of Scotland
    Helskyr na Monich 1654 *Atlas Novus* Uistus Insula
    Monach Islands 1878x1880 OS 6 inch first edn.
    Monach Islands 1973 OS Pathf
    Na h-Eileanan Monach 1996 OS Landranger

ALSO CALLED *Heisker*. *Heiskeir* is probably derived from ON *hella*, f, 'flagstone' and ON *sker*, n, 'skerry'.
    "These islands are also known as the Monach Isles, their real name in Gaelic being Eileanan Manach: Islands of the Monks. The Gaelic for monk is manach, derived from two words: math and neach, i.e., good and person (good person). Heisgeir, O.N. Bright Rock Skerry. High Skerry. Haisgeir, O.N. Heisgeir was probably known as the Monach Isles before the Vikings arrived. Haisgeir or Haesger, can also mean Wild Sea Rock. It is really a group of two main islands. They are very rocky, one is called Haisgeir Mhór – Mhór, asp. Gaelic word, mór; big. The other is Haisgeir Eagach – Eagach, Gaelic for notched. A very apt name as the outline of this island is very serrated." (MacKillop 1991: 28)

PAIBLE ~   NUS F NF738678 1 7m
    Paible 1878x1880 OS 6 inch first edn.
    Paible 1973 OS Pathf
    Paibeil 1996 OS Landranger

PAIBLESGARRY   NUS [S or F?] NF725684 1 7-15m WEF
    Paiblesgarry 1878x1880 OS 6 inch first edn.
    Paiblesgarry 1973 OS Pathf
    Paiblesgearraidh 1996 OS Landranger

LOCH PAIBLE ~   NUS W NF720685 1 0m SWF
    Loch Paible 1878x1880 OS 6 inch first edn.
    Loch Paible 1973 OS Pathf
    Loch Phaibleil 1996 OS Landranger

KYLES-PAIBLE   NUS S NF754673 1 0-8m EAF
    Kyles-paible 1878x1880 OS 6 inch first edn.
    Kyles-paible 1973 OS Pathf
    Caolas Phaibeil 1996 OS Landranger

KIRKIBOST ISLAND ~   NUS I NF756645 1 8m
    Il. Kirkabol 1654 *Atlas Novus* Æbudæ Insulæ, sive Hebrides/The Westerne Iles of Scotland
    Yl Kirk Bol 1654 *Atlas Novus* Uistus Insula
    Kirkibost Island 1878x1882 OS 6 inch first edn.

VIKING-AGE COMMUNITIES

Kirkibost Island 1976 OS Pathf
Eilean Chirceboist 1996 OS Landranger

KIRKABOL *#~   NUS Co NF7765 3 0m
Kirkabol 1654 *Atlas Novus* Uistus Insula

Water/Sea behind and East of *Kirkibost Island*.

PAIBLE   HAR S NG031992 0m
Paible 1881 OS 6 inch first edn.
Paible 1987 OS Pathf
Paibeil 1996 OS Landranger

On Taransay.

HERMETRAY ~   HAR I NF990746 1 35m
Hermodra 1654 *Atlas Novus* Uistus Insula
Hermetray 1881 OS 6 inch first edn.
Hermetray 1971 OS Pathf
Thermatraigh 1996 OS Landranger

Possible derivations from the ON personal name *Hermundr* (m, which in original form has -ar in the gen sg) or ultimately L *eremeticus*. Considering similar examples in the Sound of Harris, the ON personal name seems the most likely derivation.

"I now come to the Puritan Gale, which happened on March 16th, 1921. This was one of the worst gales that happened in an area notorious for storms. The 'Puritan', a three masted vessel of wooden construction, was on course to Scandinavia when she was driven on to the reef of Hermatray, an island on the edge of the Minch, roughly S.S.E. of Berneray. After the storm was over, Alexander MacDonald, known as Alex Beag, was lifting his lobster creels at Obsay and while tacking out to Groatay Isle he noticed two men waving weakly from the knoll, called Compass Knoll, on Hermatray. He made for this island and discovered the 'Puritan' wrecked and breaking upon the rocks. Only three of the crew were alive…" (MacKillop 1991: 11)

"There is a good landing place here on Groay for cattle. Tacksman Roderick Campbell and others throughout the years used to graze cattle here. Indeed all the islands in this area are good for grazing cattle and sheep. The Berneray crofters leave their sheep all winter on Hermatray Isle as the pasture is rich and the climate is temperate. There is a foundation of a house in Hermatray built to store salt, etc., for a fishing scheme proposed by King Charles I. Due to the civil war, this scheme miscarried." (MacKillop 1991: 59)

CHEULES YRT *#~ NUS Co NF8083 4
Cheules Yrt 1654 *Atlas Novus* Æbudæ Insulæ, sive Hebrides/The Westerne Iles of Scotland
Chevles Yrt 1654 *Atlas Novus* Uistus Insula

VIKING-AGE COMMUNITIES

Between *Pabbay* and *Griminish Point*.

BODHA AN T-SAGAIRT * HAR Co NF880785 3
   Bodha an t-Sagairt 1991 MacKillop

"Bodha an t-Sagairt – E. of the isle of Lingay, near the shore, Sea-rock of the Priest. It is alleged that all dignitaries (all dignitaries who died in the area north of Eigg) of the Old Celtic church were buried in the isle of Boreray which is west of this rock and this skerry is in the route taken, hence the name. Neil MacKillop, Borve, Berneray, 1838 to 1928, owned a boat called 'Sagart', and it is said that this rock was only known by this name after Neil struck it with his boat." (MacKillop 1991: 37)

   Note the following related passages from MacKillop:

   Boreray Burial Ground - "Rubha an Teampuill – East side of Aird a' Bhorainn. The point of land nearest Vallay Isle. The name of the area is Hamaran. Point of the Temple. Although some locals call is by this name it is really a 'Caibeal' and not a temple. The name is Caibeal Bhororaigh, Chapel of Boreray. Caibeal is a chapel or a family burial ground. The old burial-ground of the Mac Leans of Boreray is here, and the family sepulchre. The last of the MacLeans to be buried in this chapel is John MacLean, thirteenth of Boreray, who died at Drimnin, Morven, in 1821." (MacKillop 1991: 57-8)

   The following folk-etymology is also of interest - "Mo-Ruibhe Point is in G. Aird Mo-Ruibhe, said to be from St. Mulruba who was the abbot of Bangor before sailing to Scotland in 671 A.D. He or his disciples may have called here. Many places claim him as a visitor. My own opinion is that this name is from righe, the outstretched part or base of a hill or mountain, and this fits the nature of the terrain. Cf. Coire Mor Ruighe, on the mainland and other examples. Aird Mor Righe, point of the hill slope. This definition is feasible while I cannot disprove the other theory." (MacKillop 1991: 59)

References

Bannatyne Club 1854. *Origines Parochiales Scotiae: The Antiquities Ecclesiastical and Territorial of the Parishes of Scotland. Volume Second. In Two Parts. Part 1.* Edinburgh.

Gammeltoft, P 2001. 'I sauh a tour on a toft, tryelyche i-maket': on place-names in *-toft*, *-tote* and *-tobhta* from Shetland to the Isle of Man. *Nomina* 24: 17-32.

Lind, E H 1915. *Norsk-Isländska Dopnamn och Fingerade Namn från Medeltiden.* Uppsala.

MacKillop, Donald 1991. *Sea-Names of Berneray Ainmean-Mhara Bhearnaraigh.* Repr of Rocks, Skerries, Shoals and Islands in the Sound of Harris and Uist and around the island of Berneray, *Transactions of the Gaelic Society of Inverness*, vol lvi (1988-90): 428-502.

McDonald, Fr Allan 1903. The Norsemen in Uist Folklore. *Saga-Book of the Viking Club* vol 3: 413-33.

School of Scottish Studies, University of Edinburgh, PNS85/2. Recorded 8/1985. Informants: Bill Lawson, I.D.P. Stornoway, Kerry Campbell, farm manager for

Pabbay, resident Leverburgh, Harris, Neil McDonald, now resident Bearsden, Glasgow, ex-Harris: his grandfather belonged to Pabbay. Accompanying map missing.

Stahl, Anke-Beate 1999. *Place-Names of Barra in the Outer Hebrides*. Unpublished PhD, University of Edinburgh.

VIKING-AGE COMMUNITIES

PABAY (SKYE OR STRATH) PLACE-NAME INVENTORY

GUIDE TO ENTRIES
Entries formatted for the Scottish Place-Name Database, with the consultation of Simon Taylor, in the following format:

PLACE-NAME *#~[TAB][PARISH] [SITE CLASSIFICATION] [NATIONAL GRID REFERENCE] [CERTAINTY LEVEL 1-5] [ALTITUDE] [ASPECT/DRAINAGE]
    Place-name date reference (i.e. *Place-name* **1804** Heather/Hebrides)

Explanation, derivation and related material[28].

* = not listed on Ordnance Survey Pathfinder
~ = linear feature
[PARISH] = 3-letter abbreviation, e.g. STH for Strath

Site Classification Codes:

A	*Antiquity*
Co	*Coastal*
E	*Ecclesiastical*
I	*Island*
V	*Vegetation*
W	*Water (not Coastal)*

Certainty Level:

1 – certain
2 – assumed
3 – within 1km in each direction
4 – within 5km in each direction
5 – vague (whole island or parish)

Aspect/Drainage = South-West Facing (SWF), West Facing (WEF), …

---

[28] As outlined earlier, this inventory is primarily a collection of data (with an eye to the older material). Correspondingly, modern Gaelic names are generally not translated in this explanatory entry.

VIKING-AGE COMMUNITIES

Abbreviations (in chronological order)
Atlas Novus Skia = J Blaeu 1654. *Atlas Novus*. Amsterdam.

Keulen = Gerard van Keulen 1734?. *Nieuwe paskaart van de West Kust van Schotland, de Lewys Eylanden en de noord Kust van Yrland*. In I van Keulen 1734, *De Niewe Groote Ligtende Zee-Fakkel*. Location: BM, Bod, NLS, RGS.

Huddart = Joseph Huddart 1794. *A new chart of the West coast of Scotland from the point of Ardnamurchan to Cape Wrath*. In J Huddart 1794, *The North-about Navigator*, London.

Heather/Hebrides = William Heather 1804. "A new and improved chart of the Hebrides or Lewis Islands and adjacent coast of Scotland from the Mull of Cantire to Cape Wrath". Location: BM, NLS.

Thomson/Skye = John Thomson 1824. *Skye Island &c*. In John Thomson 1832, *Atlas of Scotland*, Edinburgh.

Scot W = 1886. *Scotland: West Coast*. [Admiralty Chart no 2635]. Location: NLS.

Parish information
"Strath, also known as Kilchrist in Strathsworsdale (OS Pathf. form Strath Suardal), the church was one of the 12 parish kirks of Skye (Monro, *Western Isles*, 37). The church appears as an independent parsonage in the early 15th c., but the appearance of the incumbent as a canon in 1450 would appear to indicate that the church had become a prebend of the Isles, following upon an attempt of 1433 to erect a chapter for that bishopric (*CPL* vii, 461; viii, 100; RS 289, 253; 444, 154). This attempt appears to have failed, however, and although presentations to the parsonage and vicarage continue in the 16th c., the parsonage appertained in 1561 to the abbot of Iona, while the bishop of the Isles had his customary third of the teinds (*RSS* i nos. 1115, 1719; *Coll. de Rebus Alban.*, 3)." (Cowan 1967: 190)

"Strath. Kilcrist in Askimilruby – Church of Strath called Cristiskirk – Keilchrist in Strathawradall – Kilchrist – Strath.

This parish includes the district of Skye known as Strathswordale or Strath Mhic Ionmhuinn (MacKinnon's Strath), and the islands Scalpa, Longa, Pabba, and a few of smaller size. It is bounded on the west by the Coolin (or Cuillin) hills, 3000 feet above sea level, and stretching from the head of Loch Scavaig on the south to the head of Loch Sligichan on the north. It has numerous lakes, and at its west end north from Loch Scavaig are the lake of Coiruisge (or Coriskin), studded with green islands and surrounded with steep ragged rocks, and the famous spar cave of strathaird.

…There are the remains of chapels … on the island of Pabba." (Bannatyne Club, *Origines Parochiales Scotiae* 1854: 343-6)

"Strath. The low-lying level land between hills. A strath is larger in extent than a glen, a broad valley with a river running through it. This particular strath is one of the parishes of Skye ...

The present parish of Strath was formerly known as 'Kilchrist', *Cille Chriosd*, Christ's cell or church, the old church being formerly at Loch Chriosd, near the centre of the parish. In 1833 Strath had two other places of worship.

...Four chapels, or the ruins thereof, are here, viz., Aisk, Kilbride, Kilmori, and in the island of Pabba, in Scalpa, attached to this parish, other similar ruins may be seen. But of greater interest and antiquity there stands on the modern glebe, an immense mass of granite, finely poised on a smooth level rock; this is called generally 'Clach na h-Anaid', the store of the Annat, or ... the 'Mother' church ...

Many celebrated clerics and laymen were connected with Strath from the time of Abbot McKinnon, who succeeded Columba in Iona; this abbot was drowned; an account of his death is given in the 'Queen's Wake', by Hogg.

Strath is well supplied with good stone, and is famed for marble of different hues; this marble has been in use for many centuries, and entered into the construction of many notable buildings at home and abroad; among the stones is limestone in considerable quantity, and that at Broadford, which includes an entire mountain, viz., Benn an Dubhaich, is generally called 'the Strath marble' or 'Durness limestone' ...

This district is familiarly spoken of as 'Srath nam Bo', strath of the kine, while Ossian called or named it 'Srath of the Coolins', and here, as tradition gives it, six thousand deer were slain by three thousand hounds. Another title is 'srath nam Faochag', strath of the whelks or buckies, which furnish the nick-name of the 'The Whelks' to its people. Strath share with Sleat in possessing a large number of rare ferns and other wild-growing plants, among which are the *Erinocaulon septangulare* and *Dryas octopetala*.

...The Mackinnons were also closely connected with the island of Mull, and it was to those resident there that the nickname of 'Na Faochagan' is applied ..." (Forbes 1923: 412-5)

Place-name inventory
PABAY ~   STH I NG672270 1 28m
    Paba 1654 *Atlas Novus* Skia
    Paba 1734? Keulen
    Pabbay 1794 Huddart
    Pabbay I. 1804 Heather/Hebrides [*I.* = Island]
    Pabba 1824 Thomson/Skye
    Paba 1886 Scot W
    Pabay 1881 OS 6 inch first edn.
    Pabay 1988 OS Pathf
    Pabay 1997 OS Landranger

"Pabba, Pabbay, Papa, etc. Father (monk or priest) island; Norse *pap* and *ey* or *papar*, father, etc.; Gaelic celi De ceile; Latin servi Dei, both meaning servants of God; spelled also Pabra, which is given as near Beakish, Strath, and north of Kyleakin. Pabba forms a breakwater to Broadford Bay, lies low, and is of a mossy green meadow nature. Dean Monro mentions it specially.

There are three Pabbas at least; this particular one is famed for petrified fish found on its shores, also for fossils and petrifications generally; it contains an ancient burying-ground and chapel, all in ruins." (Forbes 1923: 272)

"Pabay. 109. At the shore of Sky forsaid, lyes ane Ile callit Pabay neyre ane myle in lenthe, full of woodes, guid for fishing and a maine shelter for thieves and cut-throats, it pertains to McKynnoun." (Monro 1549: 283)

SHELL BEACH   STH Co NG675278 1 0m NOF
    Shell Beach 1988 OS Pathf
    Shell Beach 1997 OS Landranger

FORD STH W NG675277 1 8m
    Ford 1988 OS Pathf

LION ROCK   STH Co NG679275 1 0m NEF
    Lion Rock 1988 OS Pathf

CHAPEL (REMS OF)   STH AE N674265 1 0m SOF
    Chapel (Ruins of) 1882 OS 6 inch first edn.
    Chapel (rems of) 1988 OS Pathf
    Chapel 1997 OS Landranger

JETTY STH CoO NG671264 1 0m SOF
    Jetty 1988 OS Pathf
    Jetty 1997 OS Pathf

AN GOBHLACH   STH Co NG668261 1 0m SWF
    An Gobhlach 1882 OS 6 inch first edn.
    An Gobhlach 1988 OS Pathf
    An Gobhlach 1997 OS Landranger

Gaelic *gòbhlach* (Dwelly 1901) 'forked, pronged', thus 'The Forked One', probably referring to the promontory.

GRAVE YARD (DISUSED) *   STH E NG673264 2 0m SEF
    Grave Yard (Disused) 1876x1882 OS 6 inch first edn.

MOSS *~   STH V NG677269 10m
    Moss 1882 OS 6 inch first edn.

Relates to SE quarter of *Pabay*.

Surrounding sea and island names
SGEIR GOBLACH   I NG667256 1 0m
　　Sgeir Ghobhlach 1876x1882 OS 6 inch first edn.
　　Sgeir Goblach 1988 OS Pathf
　　Sgeir Gobhlach 1997 OS Landranger

References
Bannatyne Club 1854. *Origines Parochiales Scotiae: The Antiquities Ecclesiastical and Territorial of the Parishes of Scotland. Volume Second. In Two Parts. Part 1.* Edinburgh.
Cowan, I B 1967. *The Parishes of Medieval Scotland.* Scottish Record Society vol 93. Edinburgh.
Dwelly, Edward 1901. *The Illustrated Gaelic-English Dictionary.*
Forbes, Alexander Robert 1923. *Place-Names of Skye and Adjacent Islands: With Lore, Mythical, Traditional and Historical.* Paisley.
Monro, Dean Donald 1549. *A Description of the Westerne Iles of Scotland called Hybrides. Compyled by Mr Donald Monro Deane of the Iles. 1549.* In Sir Arthur Mitchell and James Toshash Clark (eds), 1908, *Geographical Collections Relating to Scotland made by Walter MacFarlane*, 3 vols, Edinburgh.

VIKING-AGE COMMUNITIES

PABBAY(S) (SOUTH UIST) PLACE-NAME INVENTORY

Guide to entries
Entries formatted for the Scottish Place-Name Database, with the consultation of Simon Taylor, in the following format:

PLACE-NAME *#~[TAB][PARISH] [SITE CLASSIFICATION] [NATIONAL GRID REFERENCE] [CERTAINTY LEVEL 1-5] [ALTITUDE] [ASPECT/DRAINAGE]
    Place-name date reference (i.e. ***Place-name* 1881 OS 6 inch first edn.**)

Explanation, derivation and related material[29].

* = not listed on Ordnance Survey Pathfinder
~ = linear feature
[PARISH] = 3-letter abbreviation, e.g. SUS for South Uist

Site Classification Codes:

F	*Field*
I	*Island*
W	*Water (not Coastal)*

Certainty Level:

1 – certain
2 – assumed
3 – within 1km in each direction
4 – within 5km in each direction
5 – vague (whole island or parish)

---

[29] As outlined earlier, this inventory is primarily a collection of data (with an eye to the older material). Correspondingly, modern Gaelic names are generally not translated in this explanatory entry.

VIKING-AGE COMMUNITIES

Abbreviations (in chronological order)
Atlas Novus Skia = J Blaeu 1654. *Atlas Novus*. Amsterdam.

Keulen = Gerard van Keulen 1734? *Nieuwe paskaart van de West Kust van Schotland, de Lewys Eylanden en de noord Kust van Yrland.* In I van Keulen 1734, *De Niewe Groote Ligtende Zee-Fakkel.* Location: BM, Bod, NLS, RGS.

Huddart = Joseph Huddart 1794. *A new chart of the West coast of Scotland from the point of Ardnamurchan to Cape Wrath.* In J Huddart 1794, *The North-about Navigator*, London.

Heather/Hebrides = William Heather 1804. "A new and improved chart of the Hebrides or Lewis Islands and adjacent coast of Scotland from the Mull of Cantire to Cape Wrath". Location: BM, NLS.

Thomson/Skye = John Thomson 1824. *Skye Island &c.* In John Thomson 1832, *Atlas of Scotland*, Edinburgh.

Scot W = 1886. *Scotland: West Coast*. [Admiralty Chart no 2635]. Location: NLS.

Parish information
"Now in the parish of South Uist, Pabbay lay in the medieval parish of Kilpeder, known also as *Kilpedire Blisen* and *Kilpheder* in Uist, the church, which was one of the five parish kirks of Uist, was an independent parsonage in 1441 but by the Reformation had been annexed to Iona. As was customary one third of the teinds pertained to the bishops of the Isles. (Monro *W.I.* 48-9; *Coll. de Rebus Alban* 3)." (Cowan 1967: 109)

"Kilpeter. Parochia de Kilpedire Blisen – Peitter's Paraochin – Keilpedder in Veist – Kilfadrik – Kilphedre.

This parish, now part of the modern parish of South Uist (which includes also Howmore and Benbecula), seems to have consisted of the district known as Kandish or the South Head of Uist, the district of Boisdale (of old Baghastil), and the islands Eriskay, Lingay, and Oronsay, and a few smaller isles, thus extending from the extreme south of Eriskay to the neighbourhood of Loch Eynort on the east and of the promontory styled Ardmichael on the west. The west side of the parish is low, flat, and sandy, the east rocky, mountainous, and indented by Loch Boisdale [where the Pabbay(s) are found]. Fresh-water lakes are numerous.

…There were chapels at Kilbride in Boisdale, and at Kildonnan and apparently also at Clachan of Branagh, Clachan Cuay, and Kirkidale, in the other and larger portion of the parish." (Bannatyne Club, *Origines Parochiales Scotiae* 1854: 365-8)

Place-name inventory
PABBAY ~   SUS I NF778195 1 14m
    Pabbay 1881 OS 6 inch first edn.

Pabbay 1976 OS Pathf
Pabaigh 1995 OS Landranger

Two islands joined by a tidal causeway at NF778196. On OS 6 inch first edn., both individually named *Pabbay*. On OS Pathf, both islands grouped as one and given the name *Pabbay*.

WELL *   SUS W NF780197 2 0m
   Well 1881 OS 6 inch first edn.

[FIELD DIVISION]   SUS F NF777198 – NF778197 1 0m
   - 1881 OS 6 inch first edn.
   - 1976 OS Pathf

[FIELD DIVISION]   SUS F NF778197 – NF779198 1 0m
   - 1881 OS 6 inch first edn.
   - 1976 OS Pathf

[FIELD DIVISION]   SUS F NF778197 – NF780198 1 0m
   - 1881 OS 6 inch first edn.
   - 1976 OS Pathf

[FIELD DIVISION]   SUS F NF778194 – NF779195 1 0-8m
   - 1881 OS 6 inch first edn.
   - 1976 OS Pathf

References

Bannatyne Club 1854. *Origines Parochiales Scotiae: The Antiquities Ecclesiastical and Territorial of the Parishes of Scotland. Volume Second. In Two Parts. Part 1.* Edinburgh.

Cowan, I B 1967. *The Parishes of Medieval Scotland.* Scottish Record Society vol 93. Edinburgh.

Monro, Dean Donald 1549. *A Description of the Westerne Iles of Scotland called Hybrides. Compyled by Mr Donald Monro Deane of the Iles. 1549.* In Sir Arthur Mitchell and James Toshash Clark (eds), 1908, *Geographical Collections Relating to Scotland made by Walter MacFarlane*, 3 vols, Edinburgh.

VIKING-AGE COMMUNITIES

PABBAY (BARRA) PLACE-NAME INVENTORY

Selected and annotated place-names drawn from:

Stahl, Anke-Beate 1999. *Place-Names of Barra in the Outer Hebrides.* **Unpublished PhD, University of Edinburgh.**

Guide to entries

Entries formatted for the Scottish Place-Name Database, largely following the system used by Anke-Beate Stahl in her PhD thesis. The phonetic transcription of each Place-name has been omitted here but is provided by Stahl in her thesis.

PLACE-NAME [TAB]   [NGR] [Site Classification] [Source]
name of a place
1823 Place-name
Alias: The Cowshed
Explanation, derivation and related material – including commentary on Stahl's analysis. (Page number of this passage from Stahl)

Site Classification Codes:

A   *Antiquity*
I   *Island*
R   *Relief*
S   *Settlement*
T   *Tidal Island*
U   *Underwater Features (Reef)*
W   *Water*
O   *Other (Quarry, Bridge)*

Sources:

ML *stands for MacLean's map of 1823, the first comprehensive map of both coastal and interior features of Barra and surrounding islands.*
SH *refers to estate plan by H Sharbau, 1901.*
OR *the place-name has been collected from an oral source and it has not survived in a written form. The spelling of the name conforms to current orthography.*
OS *place-name extracted from the OS Pathfinder map.*
* *indicates that older written forms of the name exist.*

Sound Archive for Pabbay (Barra):

SA 1958/160   Mingulay, Pabbay, Sandray – Informant: J MacLeod (Fieldwk: J Ross)
SA 1960/96/A1   Pabbay – Informant: N MacKinnon (Fieldworker: L Sinclair)
SA 1976/9   Castle Bay, Vatersay, Sandray, Pabbay, Mingulay
                 Informant: M MacAulay (Fieldworker: I A Fraser)

VIKING-AGE COMMUNITIES

Abbreviations (in chronological order and including date)

1549 Sir Donald Munro (report)

1654 Joannis Blaeu (maps):
  Atlas Novus Æbudæ Insulæ, sive Hebrides / The Westerne Iles of Scotland
  Atlas Novus Uistus Insula

1695 Martin Martin (account):
  1994 *A description of the Western Isles of Scotland circa 1695*. London.

1764 Dr John Walker (report):
  1980 *The Rev. Dr. John Walker's Report on the Hebrides of 1764 and 1771*, Margaret M McKay (ed). Edinburgh, pp 85-91.

1794a Rev Edward MacQueen (1st Statistical Account):
  Parish of Barra. In *The Statistical Account of Scotland* vol 13: 326-42.

1794b Joseph Huddart (chart):
  Joseph Huddart. *A new chart of the West coast of Scotland from the point of Arnamurchan to Cape Wrath*. In *The North-about Navigator*. London.

1805-1919 Craigston Register (register)

1823 MacLean (map):
  Map of Barra as part of John Thomson *Southern Part of the Western Isles*.

1824 MacCulloch (account):
  MacCulloch, John 1824. *The Highlands and Western Isles of Scotland*. London.

1845 Rev Alexander Nicolson (2nd Statistical Account):
  Parish of Barray. In *The New Statistical Account of Scotland* vol 14. Edinburgh, 198-217.

1854 J M Wilson (gazetteer):
  The Imperial Gazetteer of Scotland; or Dictionary of Scottish Topography. Edinburgh.

1865 Admiralty (Otter, Edye *et al*) (chart):
  Otter, Edye, *et al* Admiralty Chart no. 2474 *Hebrides or Western Isles from Barra to Scarpa Island*. Corrections in 1872.

1876 OS, scale 6 inches, cheets 59, 60, 62-70

1901 H Sharbau (estate plan)

1945 Admiralty (chart):
  Admiralty Chart 2770 *Sound of Barra*.

1992 OS Pathfinder 260, (NL58/68), scale 1:25000, "Mingulay"

1997 OS Landranger 31, scale 1:50000, "Barra and South Uist"

Parish information

"Barray. Kilbarr – Kilbarray – Kilbarra.

About the year 1734 Barray was disjoined from the parish of South Uist, to which it appears to have been united after the Reformation.

The parish of Barray, now apparently of the same extent as of old, consists of the island of Barray and upwards of twenty smaller isles, of which the chief are Bernera, Mingulay, Pabbay, Sanderay, and Wattersay on the south of Barray, and Uidhay, Flodday, Hellesay, Gighay, Fuday, and Fiaray, on the north. The whole parish is hilly, and the west coast in general rocky, and in Bernera and Mingulay the rocks rise to the height of 700 and 1400 feet. Beside Mingulay is a high rock (probably the *Scarpa Vervecum* of Buchanan) topped with luxuriant grass, to which the inhabitants of the island used to carry their sheep to feed. On the north coast of Barray is a tract of sand styled the Trayrmore or Great Sands of Barray.

...There was a chapel in each of the nine islands on the south of Barray, namely ...Pabay...

In 1549 the isles lying south of Barray, of which the largest are those nine already enumerated as having chapels, were held by the bishop of the Isles (probably of Macneill of Barray). In 1561 the five isles of Barry (meaning probably Bernera, Mingulay, Pabbay, Sanderay, and Watersay, and including the smaller isles) were the property of the same bishop. They were styled the bishop's isles, and Bernera the most southerly seems still to be known as the bishop's isle.

...In the parish are the ruins or sites of eleven hill forts, five of which are in Barray, two in Watersay, and one in each of the isles Sanderay, Pabbay, Mingalay, and Bernera.

There are also several circles of stone, and near one of them a well styled *tobbar-nam-buadh* (the well of virtues)." (Bannatyne Club, *Origines Parochiales Scotiae* 1854: 362-5)

Place-name inventory
RUBHA GREOTACH   NL589871 R OS
gravelly promontory
1901 Rubh' na Geod
The specific originates from ON *grjót*, n, 'gravel'. It appears we have a Gaelic adjective formed from the ON noun *grjót*, which has then been used to form this place-name. If that is the case it cannot be considered a Norse place-name. However, no such word appears in Dwelly (1901). (Stahl 1999: 250)

ALLANISH   NL593879 R OS
Alias: Rubha Alainis [sic]
Fr. Allan McDonald lists *Eileir-nis* and *Eile-nais* as alternative spellings (McDonald 1958: 287). If a personal name, they are corresponding variations of the ON name *Ølvir* (Lind, 1915: 1247f.) such as *Eilir*, *Aelir* and *Eiler* (Stahl 1999: 106). However, in light of the possible eel-names on Pabbay (HAR), an alternate suggestion derives the name from ON *állanes* 'eels' ness'. As with the *Pabbay* (HAR) eel-names, *Allanish* also lies on the west side of the island. However, these names may instead contain *áll*, m, 'deep, narrow channel' or 'deep valley'.

RUBH' ALAINIS   NL593881 R ML
promontory of A.
1823 Rullanish, 1865 –
Alias: Allanish
The OS use the unexpanded form *Allanish*. See *Allanish*. (Stahl 1999: 247)

AN CEARCALL   NL591873 R OR

the circle
1901 Cearcall
The OS location at NL593875 is wrong. (Stahl 1999: 116)

THE HOE   NL594873 R OS
the hill
1823 Hoemore
Alias: An t-Aonach Pabach
From ON *haugr*, m, 'hill'. (Stahl 1999: 290)

AN T-AONACH PABACH   NL594873 R OR
the Pabbay plateau
Alias: The Hoe
See Pabbay. (Stahl 1999: 128)

SLOC GLANSICH   NL5923877 W OS
Alias: Sloc an Uisge
The OS Object Name Book mentions that a man called *Glensig* fell over the cliff and drowned at this point. The *Glensig* may be a nickname meaning 'the shiny one'. If so, this name is from Eng *glance* > ScG *gleans, gleansach*. This name corresponds to the name *Sgeirean Sloc Ghleansaich* which was collected from an oral source. (Stahl 1999: 274)

SLOC AN UISGE   NL592877 W ML
freshwater gully
1823 Slockanuish
Alias: Sloc Glansich
(Stahl 1999: 272)

SYMBOL STONE   NL607876 A OS
(Stahl 1999: 287)

SUMULA   NL607873 R OS*
pebbly beach
1823 Sumulum
Compare to *Humula*. (Stahl 1999: 287) *Humula* originates from ON *hømull*, m, 'layer of pebbles' or 'beach stone'. The 'a' in the final position is of unclear origin. This derivation is possible; however, a difficulty is that ON **hømull* is not recorded independently in ON. (Stahl 1999: 212)

BÀGH BÀN   NL650922 W OS
white bay
(Stahl 1999: 135)

DÙNAN RUADH   NL613876 A OS
red little fort

(Stahl 1999: 192)

ROSINISH   NL615872 R OS*
headland of the horse
1823 Ruroshinish, 1846 Ruroshinish, 1997 Ròisinis
Alias: Rubha Phabach
A combination of ON *hrosr*, n, 'horse' and ON *nes*, n, 'headland'. (Stahl 1999: 245-6)

STEIR NL614876 W OS
"This name is applied to the narrow neck which joins Rosinish to the mainland of the island. On the north-west of this neck is a good creek and easy landing-place." OS Object Name Book, 1878 (Stahl 1999: 286)

LANDING PLACE   NL610873 W ML
(Stahl 1999: 218)

CAIRNS   NL618869 O OS
Scot *Cairn*, 'stone mound'.
(Stahl 1999: 159)

SLOC GLAMARIGEO   NL599869 W OS*
gully of ?
1823 Slockghlamerika, 1997 Sloc Glamain Gèodha
This gully is situated at the particularly steep and indented southern coastline of *Pabbay*. For possible derivations see *Sloc Lamarigeo* (Stahl 1999: 274) :

> Sloc Lamarigeo ... The specific of this tautological name may be interpreted in two different ways. The second element may either be a combination of ON hlað, 'layer', ON hamarr, 'steep hillside', and ON gjá, 'gully', resulting in a possible translation 'gully of the layered steep hillside' and in its combination of ON hlað and hamarr be related to G làimhrig, 'landing-place'. Located at the steep and indented western coast ... this gully is imbedded in high cliffs but is almost certainly unsuitable for use as a landing-place. Alternatively the specific may derive from ON hrafn, m, 'raven' as in Eysteinsson's Ramerigeo (see Eysteinsson 1992: 35). He traces ON hrafn back to hramn according to the morphological rule after which n becomes r after m. Eysteinsson mentions places in the Western and Northern Isles which are called 'raven gully' such as Ramnaigea (see MacAulay 1972: 333), Ramnagio (see Jakob Jakobsen, 'The Dialect and Place-Names of Shetland', Two Popular Lectures, 1897, p.98.) and Hrafnagjá which appears at least twice in Iceland (see Eysteinsson 1992: 36). The change from the initial sound /r/ to /l/ is common in certain parts of the Western Isles and would support the second derivation. (Stahl 1999: 275-6)

For a recent discussion of *làimhrig* (suggesting that it is a Pictish loan-word into Gaelic), see R A V Cox, 1997, 'Modern Scottish Gaelic Reflexes of Two Pictish Words: *pett* and *lannerc*', *Nomina* 20: 47-58.

RUBH' A' CHÀRNAIN   NL606868 R OS*

promontory of the stony ground
1823 Rucharnan
(Stahl 1999: 246)

PABBAY   NL602875 I OS*
hermit's island
1549 Pabay, 1695 Pabay, 1764 Pabay, 1794b I. Pabba, 1807 Pabbay, 1824 Pabba, 1845 Pabbay, 1848 Pabbay I.
A combination of ON *papi*, m, 'hermit' and ON *øy*, f, 'island'. (Stahl 1999: 238)
   "Pabay. 134. Besydes the Isle of Megaly to the North northeist lyes ane Ile callit Pabay ane mile lange, manurit. In it is guid take of fisch, it pertaines to the Bishope of the Isles." (Monro 1549: 286)

BÀGH NA H-AONAICH   NL596868 W ML
bay of the flat-topped height
1823 Beirranahina, 1846 Berranahind
See *Am Bàgh*. (Stahl 1999: 137):
   Am Bàgh ... the bay G bàgh, m, from ON vágr, 'bay'. (Stahl 1999: 108)

AN CNOC DUBH   NL608878 R SH
the black hill
This name mentioned on Sharbau's estate plan as *Cnoc Dhu*. (Stahl 1999: 116)

BOGHA CHIGEIN AN EAR NL618873 U OR
eastern scat reef
Alias: Bogha Chigein Beag
For the element *bogha*, see *Bogh' a' Bhàig*. (Stahl 1999: 150):
   Bogh' a' Bhàig ... G bogha, m, a loan from ON boði, m, 'reef'. (Stahl 1999: 148)

BOGHA CHIGEIN BEAG   NL618873 U OR
small scat reef
Alias: Bogha Chigein an Ear
For the element *bogha*, see *Bogh' a' Bhàig*. (Stahl 1999: 151):
   Bogh' a' Bhàig ... G bogha, m, a loan from ON boði, m, 'reef'. (Stahl 1999: 148)

BOGHA CHIGEIN A DEAS NL617866 U OR
southern scat reef
Alias: Bogha Chigein Mór
Dwelly (1901). For the element *bogha*, see *Bogh' a' Bhàig*. (Stahl 1999: 150):
   Bogh' a' Bhàig ... G bogha, m, a loan from ON boði, m, 'reef'. (Stahl 1999: 148)

BOGHA CHIGEIN MÓR   NL617866 U OR

large scat reef
Alias: Bogha Chigein a Deas
For the element *bogha*, see *Bogh' a' Bhàig*. (Stahl 1999: 151):
> Bogh' a' Bhàig ... G bogha, m, a loan from ON boði, m, 'reef'. (Stahl 1999: 148)

BOGHA NÉILL AN TÀILLEIR   NL590876 U OR
sunken rock of Neil (son of) the tailor
Alias: Sgeir Néill an Tàilleir, Sgeirean Sloc Ghleansaich
For the element *bogha*, see *Bogh' a' Bhàig*. (Stahl 1999: 151):
> Bogh' a' Bhàig ... G bogha, m, a loan from ON boði, m, 'reef'. (Stahl 1999: 148)

G *tàilleir*, m, a loan from Eng *tailor*. (Stahl 1999: 153)

SGEIR NÉILL AN TÀILLEIR   NL590876 I OR
skerry of Neil (son of) the tailor
Alias: Bogha Néill an Tàilleir, Sgeirean Sloc Ghleansaich
G *tàilleir*, m, a loan from Eng *tailor*. (Stahl 1999: 264)

SGEIREAN SLOC GHLEANSAICH   NL590876 I OR
skerries of S.
Alias: Sgeir Néill an Tàilleir, Bogha Néill an Tàilleir
See *Sloc Glansich*. (Stahl 1999: 265-6)

CNOC TUATH   NL598877 R SH
north hill
(Stahl 1999: 176)

CREAG   NL608880 R SH
rock
1910 Craig
(Stahl 1999: 178)

BISHOP'S ISLES   NL560830 I OR*
1695 Bishop's Isles, 1794b The Bishop's Isles
There is some confusion as to what islands are included in this term. *Berneray*, *Mingulay* and *Pabbay* are always included in this group, sometimes *Sandray* too, and on inaccurate maps sometimes even *Vatersay*. (Stahl 1999: 147)

BOGHANNAN AN RUBHA PHABAICH   NL617867 U OR
sunken rocks of R.
This place consists of two reefs of which one is located at the NGR indicated. The second reef is marked at NL615871. For the element *bogha*, see *Bogh' a' Bhàig*. (Stahl 1999: 155):
> Bogh' a' Bhàig ... G bogha, m, a loan from ON boði, m, 'reef'. (Stahl 1999: 148)

See also *Rubha Phabach*. (Stahl 1999: 155)

RUBHA PHABACH   NL615872 R OR
Pabbay point
Alias: Rosinish
This place is located on *Pabbay*. See *Pabbay*. (Stahl 1999: 253)

GREÒTAL   NL591871 R OR
gravel mound
1823 Greotas
A variation of this name, *Na Greotan*, is given for NGR NL593869. It is likely to apply to the same place. ON *grjót*, n, 'gravel', is a popular element in Norwegian place-names. *Greòtal* ... A combination of ON *grjót*, n, 'gravel', 'stone', and ON *hóll*, f, 'mound' ... See also Stemshaug (1976: 133). (Stahl 1999: 208)

HOGH BEAG NL598875 R SH
small hill
1901 Hoe Beg
See *The Hoe*. (Stahl 1999: 211):
   From ON haugr, m, 'hill'. (Stahl 1999: 290)

NA SLOCAN DUBHA   NL599882 W OR
the black gullies
Malcolm MacAulay locates this place-name east of *Sròn Lithinis*. (Stahl 1999: 235)

SRÒN LITHINIS   NL602884 R OR
promontory of L.
The first vowel in *Lithinis* is pronounced with a hiatus /ii/. See *Leehinish*. (Stahl 1999: 284):
   ... Leanish, 'shelter headland' ...The generic is ON nes, n, 'headland'. A number if interpretation attempts have been made for the specific. The ON adj. Lang, 'long', appears unlikely as there are longer headlands in the area. Borgstrøm suggests ON loegir, m, 'the sea', for 'headland with an anchoring place' (Campbell, 1936: 291). A geographically possible derivation is from ON hlið, f, ['hillside'] (Cox, 1987: 209) which is geographically correct and appears to be most likely. (Stahl 1999: 221)

SLOC PHABAIGH   NL608872 W OR
gully of P.
See Pabbay. (Stahl 1999: 279)

SRÒN AN RUBHA   NL618868 R OR
promontory of the point
(Stahl 1999: 283)

SRÒN BHEAG AN T-SRUTHA   NL589871 R OR

little promontory of the current
(Stahl 1999: 283)

STILL NL592877 S OR
In G *still* means 'spout of any liquid', 'cataract' or 'torrent'. The name designates an area in west *Pabbay* at the confluence of two streams which are likely to have inspired the namer. The remoteness of the valley and the availability of fresh water were ideal for the illegal production of whisky which is said to have taken place at this location and which is said to have never been discovered by officials. At this point in time it is impossible to say whether the location was named after G *still* for 'torrents' or after the Scots word 'still' (which is the origin of ScG *stalla*). (Stahl 1999: 286)

THE BANKS   NL613873 U OR
The banks
(Stahl 1999: 290)

TRÀIGH PHABAIGH   NL609874 R OR
beach of P.
See *Pabbay*. (Stahl 1999: 299)

Surrounding sea and island names
LINGAY   NL603897 I OS*
heather island
1549 Lingay, 1654 Linga, 1764 Lingay, 1794b Linga I., 1823 Lingay, 1824 Longa, 1846 Lingay, 1848 Linga, 1854 -, 1865 Lingay
A combination of ON *lyng*, n, 'heather' and ON *øy*, f, 'island'. (Stahl 1999: 222)

GREANAMUL   NL620898 I OS*
green island
1549 Gigarun?, 1654 Grialum, 1794b Creanmul, 1823 Grianimul, 1854 Grianimul, 1865 Grianameal, 1945 Greanamul
In this name the first element is likely to be derived from ON *grœnn*, 'green'. The generic originates in ON *múli*, m, 'headland', 'large rock, surrounded by the sea'. (Stahl 1999: 207)

INNER HEISKER   NL585867 I OS
inner flagstone skerry
1901 Inner Hesker
Alias: Na Dubh Sgeirean
Borgstrøm derives the name from ON *hellu-sker*, 'flagstone skerry' (Campbell 1936: 294). Sommerfelt finds this derivation improbable. Cox lists the name *Theisker* which he derives from ON *heið*, f, 'heath' and *sker*, n, 'skerry'. Arne Kruse emphasizes that skerries in the ON sense of the word do not show any signs of vegetation. The meaning 'flagstone skerry' appears to be the most likely choice. (Stahl 1999: 213)

NA DUBH SGEIREAN   NL585867 I OR
the black skerries
Alias: Inner Heisker
G *sgeir*, f, a loan from ON *sker*, n, 'skerry'. (Stahl 1999: 232)

OUTER HEISKER   NL573867 I OS
outer H.
1901 Outer Hesker
Alias: Heisker, Sgeir nan Ròn
See *Inner Heisker*. (Stahl 1999: 238)

HEISKER   NL573867 I OS*
flagstone skerry
1654 Heyskyra, 1846 Heisker, 1865 Hesker
Alias: Outer Heisker, Sgeir nan Ròn
The name is probably derived from ON *hella*, f, 'flagstone' and ON *sker*, n, 'skerry'. Cox's derivation of *Theisger* from ON *heið* (Cox 1987: 227) is not applicable, as this skerry has neither heather nor peat, nor any other obvious signs of vegetation. (Stahl 1999: 211)

SGEIR NAN RÒN   NL573867 I OR
skerry of the seals
Alias: Outer Heisker, Heisker
(Stahl 1999: 264)

MINGULAY NL558831 I OS*
big island
1549 Megaly, 1654 Megala, 1695 Micklay, 1794 Mingula, 1794a Mingalay, 1794b Mingalla I., 1805 Mingalay, 1824 Mingala, 1845 Mingalay, 1846 Mingulay, 1848 Mingalay I. 1854 Mingala, 1865 Mingulay
Borgstrøm suggests *Mi'ulaidh* for G spelling and *Mikiley* for ON. He translates the name as 'big isle' for ON *mikil*, 'big', which later was weakened to /g/. The /u/ sound cannot be accounted for so that the meaning is not entirely certain. However, the -ng- is crucial, because it leads to 'the -u-sound' developing, and also weakens to -gh- in Hebridean Gaelic: thus ON *mikil* 'big' is not possible. The generic originates from ON *øy*, f, 'island'. *Mingulay* is the largest and highest of the islands south of Barra. (Stahl 1999: 229)

BERNERAY NL556801 I OS*
Bjorn's island
1549 Berneray, 1654 Bernera, 1794a Berneray, 1794b Berneray, 1823 Bernera, 1840 Berneray, 1848 Bernera I., 1854 Bernera, 1865 –
Borgstrøm discusses this name in Campbell (1936: 289). He suggests *Bearnaraidh* as G spelling and *Bjarnarey* as ON spelling. The specific is derived from ON *bjørn*, m, 'bear' or from the ON personal name *Bjørn* (ON *biarnar* / *Biarnar*, gen sg of *björn* / *Björn*). The generic is derived from ON *ey*, f, 'island'. (Stahl 1999: 146)

SOUND OF PABBAY   NL613888 W OS*
sound of P.
1823 -, 1848 –
See *Pabbay*. (Stahl 1999: 282)

SOUND OF MINGULAY   NL583859 W OS*
sound of M.
1823 -, 1865 -
See *Mingulay*. (Stahl 1999: 282)

SGEIR AN T-SALAINN   NL601882 T ML
salt skerry
1823 Skerant, 1901 Sgeir Antallin
The 1823 entry shows only the first part of this place-name, the specific has been forgotten. (Stahl 1999: 258)

Selected names from the region
HECLA   NL558823 R OS*
high mountain
1823 Heclavore, 1865 Hecla
Stahl suggests this name was directly imported from Iceland where *Hecla* is the name of a famous (and active) volcano. It contains the ON adj. *hár*, 'high' and ON *klettr*, m, 'mountain'. The MacLean map of 1823 indicates the existance of *Heclaveg* and *Heclavore*. (Stahl 1999: 210) However, if *Hecla* is not a name-form found in Scandinavia itself, then the Icelandic *Hekla* may either have arisen alongside the Hebridean *Heclas* (on Barra and South Uist) or could have been imported to southern Iceland from the Hebrides.

CAVE NL606895 R OS
(Stahl 1999: 168) [on Lingay]

CROIS AN T-SUIDHEACHAIN   NL566828 R OS6"
Cross of the seat
"This name applies to a small spot with some trace of what appears to have been a building and is traditionally believed to have been a place of worship erected by a disciple of St. Columba. A few stones only are remaining." OS Object Name Book. (Stahl 1999: 183) [on Mingulay]

ST. COLUMBA'S CHAPEL NL566834 A OS*
Even in 1877 when the OS undertook their survey, the site of *St. Columba's chapel* could no longer be clearly identified. (Stahl 1999: 285) [on Mingulay]

RUBHA PHABACH NL640904 R OR
point of the Pabbay men(?)

1823 Ard Phabbach
Alias: Aird Pabbach
This place is located on *Sandray* facing *Pabbay*. It may have been the landing-place of the *Pabbay* men. See *Pabbay*. (Stahl 1999: 253)

AIRD PABBACH   NL640904 R OS*
Pabbay headland
1823 Ard Phabbach
Alias: Rubha Pabach
This headland is located on *Sandray* facing *Pabbay*. See *Pabbay*. (Stahl 1999: 104)

References

Bannatyne Club 1854. *Origines Parochiales Scotiae: The Antiquities Ecclesiastical and Territorial of the Parishes of Scotland. Volume Second. In Two Parts. Part 1.* Edinburgh.

Borgstrøm, Carl Hj 1936. The Norse Place-Names of Barra. In Campbell (ed) *The Book of Barra*, pp. 287-95.

Borgstrøm, Carl Hj 1937. The Dialect of Barra in the Outer Hebrides. *Norsk Tidskrift for Sprogvidenskap* vol 8. Oslo.

Campbell, John Lorne (ed) 1936. *The Book of Barra*. London.

Cox, Richard A V 1987. *Place-names of the Carloway Registry, Isle of Lewis.* Unpublished PhD thesis, University of Glasgow.

Dwelly, Edward 1901. *The Illustrated Gaelic-English Dictionary.*

Eysteinsson, Oddgeir 1992. *Norse Settlement-Names of North Harris.* Unpublished MLitt thesis, University of Aberdeen.

Lind, E H 1915. *Norsk-Isländska Dopnamn och Fingerade Namn från Medeltiden.* Uppsala.

MacAulay, Donald 1972. Studying the Pace-Names of Bernera. *Transactions of the Gaelic Society of Inverness* vol 47: 313-37.

McDonald, Fr Allan 1958. *Gaelic Words and Expressions from South Uist and Eriskay.* John Lorne Campbell (ed). Dublin.

Monro, Dean Donald 1549. *A Description of the Westerne Iles of Scotland called Hybrides. Compyled by Mr Donald Monro Deane of the Iles. 1549.* In Sir Arthur Mitchell and James Toshash Clark (eds), 1908, *Geographical Collections Relating to Scotland made by Walter MacFarlane*, 3 vols, Edinburgh.

Stahl, Anke-Beate 1999. *Place-Names of Barra in the Outer Hebrides.* Unpublished PhD, University of Edinburgh.

Stemshaug, Ola 1976. *Namn i Noreg, 3rd ed.* Oslo.

CHAPTER FOUR
Viking-Age communities?

Discussion of toponymic inventory

As stated earlier, study of the *Pap*-name distribution across the Western Isles suggests important conclusions. The *Pab(b)ay* names are Norse, and a form of Old Norse was spoken in those islands until, at least, the thirteenth century. Norse speakers must have given these names sometime during this period. As Norse names, *Pab(b)ays* and *Paibles* occur in a regular distribution across the Western Isles, respecting modern regional divisions: the Barra islands, South Uist, Harris/North Uist, the Uig area of Lewis, and the Skye area each have one *Pab(b)ay*[30]. Furthermore, when the *Paibles* and other *Pap*-names are included, the population centres in the Stornoway area, Taransay and neighbouring Harris, southwest-facing Uist and Rum are each found to have a *Pap*-name. Most populated areas of the 'Long Island', Skye and Rum have a *Pab(b)ay* name – and if not, then probably a *Paible* or other *Pap*-name. This distribution of the name element suggests a consistent role for these *Pap*-places within the Norse-speaking regional structure or administration.

The previous chapter's catalogue of mostly minor names provides new information with which to test and refine ideas drawn from the large-scale analysis discussed above. Expanding upon that discussion, preliminary survey suggests 20-30% of names from *Pab(b)ay* islands are Norse[31]. Illustrated in table 5, the proportion of Norse names between these islands is remarkably similar (though the Pabay (STH) sample is very small).

---

[30] Note, however, that the South Uist *Pabbay* is the name given to two islands.
[31] The exception is the Loch Boisdale Pabbay. These islands have only one surviving name, which is Norse.

Island (PARISH)	Number of names	Percentage of names derived from Norse
Pabbay (HAR)	40	*30%*
Pabay (STH)	5	*20%*
Pabbay (SUS)	1	-
Pabbay (BRR)	30	*25%*

Table 5 Preliminary survey of Pab(b)ay names derived from Norse. Numbers are approximate and exclude marine features. Note that names which derive directly from Norse (i.e. coined by Norse-speakers) are separated out from those younger names which contain Norse loan-words in Gaelic, and were therefore coined by Gaelic-speakers. This analysis was carried out by Simon Taylor.

Initial analysis of the inventory material, carried out by Simon Taylor, explores primarily these Norse names from the island (Taylor 2002). Regarding the 25% Norse names from Pabbay (BRR), the following observations may be made:

- Names are almost exclusively topographical or relate to natural resources. The *Allanish* name (?'eels ness') may imply that eels were potentially an important resource on the island's northwest coast. (Alternatively – and more plausibly – *Allanish* may instead contain *áll*, meaning 'deep, narrow channel' or 'deep valley'.)
- The only domesticated animal referred to is the horse (*Rosinish* < **hrossa nes* 'horses' nes').
- Aside from the island's *Pap*-name, none of the Norse names are ecclesiastical. (Nor indeed are the Gaelic names.)

In comparison, the following observations may be made from the 30% Norse names of Pabbay (HAR):

- Most of the names whose etymology is understood are topographical or relate to natural resources. Heather is noted by the name *Lingay* (*ling* 'heather' + *á* 'river, burn') whereas eels may be referred to in the name *Alarip Bay* (? *áll* 'eel' + *hóp* 'bay'), again on the island's northwest coast. (As with *Allanish*, *Alarip Bay* may instead contain *áll* 'deep, narrow channel' or 'deep valley'.) That eels were a longstanding resource may be suggested by the Gaelic name *Loch na h-Easgainn* 'loch of the eel' on the island's west coast. (However, this name may instead be founded upon a specific event – otherwise we might expect the name form **Loch nan Easgann*, 'loch of the eel<u>s</u>'.)
- *Rosikie* may contain ON *hross* 'horse' and thus be comparable to *Rosinish* above. Alternatively, this word could contain Gaelic (or Pictish) *ros* 'peninsula'. If this is the case, then the addition of the explanatory *rubha* 'promontory, point' in the modern name *Rubha Rosagaidh* means this name is of an older stratum than the majority of Gaelic names on the island.[32]

---

[32] In his study of western Lewis names, Richard Cox discusses this older stratum of names (Cox 2002: 107, 114-8).

- One pastoral name survives, *Quinish* (*kví* 'cattle or sheep fold' + *nes*). This area of the island may have experienced continuity of pastoral use until the modern period: a sheepfold was also noted near Teampull Mhóire in 1881.[33]
- Aside from the island's *Pap*-names, none of the Norse names are ecclesiastical.

Additionally, the island's *Pabbay* name suggests that *Teampull Mhóire*'s alternate name *Teampull an t-Sagairt* 'Church of the priest' (from an oral collection recorded in 1985) deserves further investigation. Comparable analysis is not possible for the remaining Strath and South Uist islands: they have only one surviving Norse name, that of the island itself.

In short, the *Pab(b)ay* name inventory provides new data. One avenue for exploring this data (that taken here) was to concentrate upon the Norse name material. The first discovery was that Norse names are largely topographical or relate to natural resources – they do not contain habitative elements (e.g. the *býli*-element 'farm, settlement'). In other words, these names do not explicitly refer to human habitation. Rather than suggesting Norse speakers did not settle on the island, however, the lack of habitative names may result from these islands having insufficient habitable area to permit secondary settlement (as secondary settlement names more often contain habitative elements). Secondly, the two potential Norse eel-names may relate to exploitation of this resource by Norse speakers – perhaps along the west coasts of the Hebridean 'Long Island'. The later Gaelic eel-name on the west coast of Pabbay (HAR) may support the idea that this animal resource was longlasting. Though *sult easgann* 'eel-fat' was used in the islands, an unresolved question is whether eels were a *resource* or a *problem* for people trying to fish for other varieties of marine animals.[34] (Another problem is that these Norse 'eel-names' may instead be topographical names.) Thirdly, domesticated animal-names are rare, with only two or three refering to horse and either cattle or sheep – only the latter in the context of an animal-fold. Lastly, no Norse ecclesiastical names were to be found on the islands.

The Old Norse stratum of names is relatively easily dated to c. AD 800-1300(?), whereas a few Gaelic- or Pictish-origin names may be of this age or older (e.g. Rosikie) and the remaining Gaelic, Scots and English names are younger. Several topics for further research emerge. These include: the older stratum of Gaelic represented by the *Rosikie* name; the uncertain antiquity of the 'priest' element in the *Teampull an t-Sagairt* name; and the potentially continuous practice, since the Norse period, of pastoralism in the *Quinish/Teampull Mhóire/Teampull an t-Sagairt* area – and therefore the area's suitability for field investigation of soil use and of settlement history. This initial analysis of the name catalogue provides some background to assessing the role that these islands played within the Norse-speaking regional structure. The work presented here is a start: toponymic inventory of the Hebridean *Pab(b)ay* islands contributes new data which raises questions regarding these places – one may expect a larger study to contextualise some of these. One immediate question is whether these

---

[33] Cox describes how the Norse name material in the Carloway area of western Lewis "shows a settled population whose influence in land use, husbandry, fishing and other occupations is seen…" (Cox 2002: 109).

[34] For lore and vocabulary on the conger eel (*easgann mhara* or 'see-eel') see A R Forbes' treatment (Forbes 1923: 359).

islands are different from the surrounding areas. A further question is how *Pap*-islands relate to nearby place-names with ecclesiastical associations, such as the *Monach Islands*[35] or *Bodha an t-Sagairt*[36]. One way of exploring these questions would be to inventory *entire* regions containing *Pap*-names (as Stahl has done for the Barra islands), and then to compare the name environments of *Pap*-places to that of their larger regions.

Pap-names reflect the settlement of early Christian Gaels before the Viking Age.
Fisher has recently pointed to the co-incidence of *Pap*-names with early Christian sculpture sites (Fisher 2002), and a number of the 'surrounding' and 'selected' names in the catalogue demonstrate the early Christian associations of these areas. However, the hypothesis outlined above requires one to deny the apparently firm datum that *Pap*-names are neither Gaelic nor Pictish names, but Norse: probably a loan word from Gaelic, but nevertheless a Norse word. Furthermore, the catalogue of minor names from these islands demonstrates that the vast majority of the smaller-scale names were given by Norse-speakers, or by more recent Gaelic-, Scots- and English-speakers. In other words, these Norse-period (or younger) names cannot be older than the Viking Age, and thus cannot reasonably be used in locating *earlier* settlements of Christian communities. One attempt to surmount this difficulty proposes that early Scandinavian colonists applied *Pap*-names to recently abandoned sites formerly occupied by early Christian Gaels (Fellows-Jensen 1996: 116). The rebuttal of this idea has been set out as follows, with reference to Scotland's Northern Isles:

> Why should it be more relevant to name abandoned *papar* sites than abandoned *pettar* [Pictish or indigenous] sites, the latter often being more distinctive with their broch structures? (Gammeltoft 2003: 94)

In other words, if sites related to the indigenous population of the presumably Pictish-speaking Northern Isles are almost completely lacking *Pettar*-names, then it is difficult to support the proposal that numerous *Pap*-names identify abandoned (and perhaps unremarkable) sites related to potentially marginal communities of early Christian Gaels. Furthermore, Gammeltoft suggests that the evidence from the Northern Isles (presumably also applicable to the Western Isles[37]) encourages the idea that:

> ...*papar* lived alongside Scandinavians ... for a prolonged period. This fits well with the fact that a large number of *papar* sites are associated with post-Viking Age chapels or graveyards, which presupposes a prolonged period of Christian worship at these sites. Whether this means a continuous clerical presence from pre-Viking Age times or not is uncertain. However, if this is the case, then the presence of the Christian *papar* might well represent attempts at converting the heathen Scandinavians. Judging from the many Christian Scandinavians from Scotland, who, according to *Landnámabók*, settled in

---

[35] See Pabbay (HAR).
[36] See Pabbay (HAR).
[37] The spirit of this argument should also apply to the Western Isles, regardless of whether they were largely Pictish-speaking or, as Cox believes, Gaelic-speaking before Norse colonisation in that area (Cox 2002: 107, 114-8).

Iceland only a couple of generations after settlement of the Northern and Western Isles of Scotland, they seem to have been fairly successful. (Gammeltoft 2003: 94)

In support of Gammeltoft's theory of prolonged coexistence, one may draw on the onomastic truism that place-names are often coined by neighbouring groups. England's many *Denbys* are a clear example. For these names for isolated 'Dane's farms' seem to have been given not by the farms' Scandinavian residents but by their English-speaking neighbours (Gammeltoft 2004b: 44). However, even if this were the circumstance in which *Pap*-names arose, the hypothesis under consideration would remain implausible. Certainly, it is possible that settlements of early Christian Gaels did continue into the Viking Age on *Pab(b)ay* islands. However it is also possible these names are related to an unconnected Viking Age religious movement or even a product of the contact situation itself – perhaps on an earlier Christian site, or perhaps not. In short, these names are indubitably Norse, and were applied by Norse-speakers in areas of Scandinavian colonisation. To propose that they reflect settlement of early Christian Gaels *before* the Viking Age would be to argue beyond the limits of the place-name material. The minor name patterns on these islands illustrate these limitations: the vast majority of names date to the Norse period or more recent centuries. Simply put, ON *Pap*-names need not be related to pre-Viking Age communities of early Christian Gaels.

EITHER: *Pap-names are retrospective names given by Old Norse speakers in the late ninth/tenth century or the twelfth century.*
OR: *Pap-names reflect the character of the earliest Norse settlement.*
In Chapter One it was suggested that *Papaey- and *Papabýli-names had lost their medial vowel (in this case the middle 'a') through the Old Norwegian syncope, producing *Papey* and triggering the phonotaxis which produced *Papýli*. These changes must have occurred in a Norse-speaking environment and preceded later transformations of these names into Scots and Gaelic, which resulted in the modern *Pab(b)ays*, *Papa(s)*, *Paibles* and *Papils* (Gammeltoft 2004b: 41). Gammeltoft provides a succinct description of the Old Norwegian syncope:

> Syncope is popularly speaking a means of shortening multi-syllabic words and names by a syllable and it probably takes place owing to frequent use of the linguistic element in question. …it is important to note that syncope does not take place in the coining process of a name but it is solely the result of frequent use of the coinage. (Gammeltoft 2004b: 42)

If Gammeltoft is right about this, the loss of the medial 'a' in *Pap*-names, was the product of frequent use of these names. Precise dating of the Old Norwegian syncope is difficult, though it may be demonstrated to have already taken place by the time of the earliest Old Norse manuscripts – i.e. before AD 1150. In other words, these *Pap*-names must, on linguisitic grounds, have been coined well before AD 1150 *at the latest* – and have been "well-established and often-used place-names prior to the time when the Old Norwegian syncope came into force" (Gammeltoft 2004b: 42).

From his work on *Papa Stronsay*, Lowe put forward the idea that the founding of twelfth-century ecclesiastical structures led to 'retrospective' naming of *Pap*-places

(Lowe 2002: 95). However, the linguistic evidence outlined above argues against the suggestion that *Pap*-names are twelfth-century 'retrospective' coinages. Additionally, the absence of any Norse ecclesiastical names from the catalogued islands (aside from the *Pab(b)ay* name itself) is at odds with the 'retrospective naming' idea. Furthermore, if this ecclesiastical name form were late, then one might expect that *Pap*-names be concentrated in areas important for the Church in that later period, as Lowe proposed for Orkney. In the Icelandic case, this should suggest that *Pap*-names would occur in the surroundings of the bishop's seats of Skálholt (in the south) or Hólar (in the north). However, the Icelandic examples of these names occur elsewhere on the island, clustered in the southeast. An equivalent Hebridean scenario would see important centres for late Viking Age Christianity, such as Iona, with a *Pap*-name. But if that was the case, it has not survived[38]. Therefore both linguistic and historical arguments may be levelled against the proposal of twelfth-century 'retrospective' naming.

Another idea to be reckoned with is MacDonald's suggestion of late ninth- and early tenth-century 'retrospective' coining of *Pap*-names. He argued that "the restricted range of forms common to all areas, the unspecified nature of the names as place-names, and also their numbers and distribution – make me think ... they were coined and applied retrospectively [in the late ninth and tenth centuries]" (MacDonald 2002: 21). Though Viking Age 'retrospective' naming is a possibility, further analysis of the place-name material argues against this. To elaborate, the first names of Scandinavian origin in the north Atlantic area are thought to be major topographical names, containing coastal, headland and river names such as *-fjörður* 'firth, bay', *-ey* 'island' and *-nes* 'ness, headland', whereas generic settlement names, such as those containing *-býli*, are understood to be marginally later. Over twenty *Pap*-names contain elements denoting major topographical features and roughly a dozen names denote settlement (the *-býli* names), which suggests that *Pap*-names may be among the earliest Scandinavian names in the north Atlantic area. This apparently robust assumption refutes the idea that these names were "coined and applied retrospectively" (Gammeltoft 2004b: 43). Note that the catalogue also identifies most of the Norse minor names as topographical, which is consistent with the naming scenario outlined above.

The third hypothesis, that *Pap*-names reflect the character of earliest Norse settlement, is the best fit. Given that *Pap*-names are Norse names and were transformed by the Old Norwegian syncope sometime before AD 1150, it may be argued on linguistic grounds that these names were coined within the period c. AD 800-1100. Given that name elements denoting major topography and settlement are thought to be the first names of Scandinavian origin in the north Atlantic area, the predominance of major topography and settlement-denoting elements in *Pap*-names (and the catalogued *Pap*-island names) points to their origin in the earliest period of Scandinavian settlement. Taken together then, the linguistic and place-name evidence suggests strongly that *Pap*-names reflect earliest Norse settlement.

---

[38] Admittedly, *Pap*-names do appear in proximity to some cross sculpture sites – but this sculpture is mostly earlier (i.e. of early Christian date).

CONCLUSIONS AND FURTHER PROBLEMS

This book has proposed important refinements to our understanding of the use of *pap*-element place-names. *Pap*-names are Norse names and may be among the earliest Scandinavian-origin names in the north Atlantic area. As Norse names, they are not directly related to early Christian settlement *before* the Viking Age. However, an indirect relationship remains possible and may be suggested by potentially early ecclesiastical structure and cross sculpture at or near *Pap*-sites (Lowe 2002; Fisher 2002). Nevertheless, the contention made here is that, on their own, *Pap*-names should not be seen as remembering early Christian settlement *before* the Viking Age, but should be interpreted as reflecting the earliest Scandinavian colonisation of the north Atlantic area. In short, this book stressed how *Pap*-names are *Old Norse* (not *Old Irish*) names, and that Hebridean *Pab(b)ay* islands underscore the ill-defined – but real – relationship between the area's Norse-speakers and early Christian communities.

When cast against the backdrop of strong early Christian associations for the Hebrides, the name catalogue raises further questions of some importance. Two such problems may be mentioned: what is the reason for the absence of Norse ecclesiastical names amongst the catalogued material (except for the *Pap*-island names)? And, does the rarity of names older than the Norse stratum suggest a change in user group with the Norse period? One direction for future research on Hebridean *Pap*-islands would be to expand inventory coverage to regions larger than a single island in order, first of all, to compare that region's names with the island's names and, secondly, to compare name distributions between regions. Such a strategy for future work may help evaluate whether *Pap*-islands indeed played a common or established role in the Norse period. Returning to the large-scale distribution, a final further problem to consider is why *Pap*-names are regularly distributed in the Scottish islands, but rare and clustered in the Faroe Islands and Iceland.

REFERENCES

Ahronson, K. 2002. *Unpublished Report: Pabbay Place-name Inventory: Including the Pab(b)ay Islands of Harris, Skye/Strath, South Uist, and Barra in the Western Isles of Scotland.*

—. forthcoming. *Claiming a Wilderness: Atlantic Gaels and the Island Norse.*

Anderson, A.O. & M.O. Anderson (eds & trans.) 1991. *Adomnan's Life of Columba.* Oxford.

Anderson, A.O. (ed. & trans.) 1922. *Early Sources of Scottish History AD 500 to 1286: Volume I.* Edinburgh.

Beauvois, E. 1875. La découverte du Nouveau Monde par les Irlandais et les premières traces du Christianisme en Amérique avant l'an 1000. *Congrès international des américanistes* **1**, 41-93.

Benediktsson, J. (ed.) 1968. *Íslendingabók Landnámabók.* Reykjavík: Hið Íslenzka Fornritafélag.

Charles-Edwards, T. 1976. The social background to Irish *peregrinatio. Celtica* **XI**, 43-59.

Cox, R.A.V. 2002. *The Gaelic Place-names of Carloway, Isle of Lewis: Their Structure and Significance.* Dublin: School of Celtic Studies, Dublin Institute for Advanced Studies.

Crawford, B. (ed.) 2002. *The Papar in the North Atlantic: Environment and History. The Proceedings of a day conference held on 24th February 2001. The 'Papar' Project. Volume 1.* (St John's House Papers No 10). St Andrews: The Committee for Dark Age Studies, University of St Andrews.

Cunliffe, B. 2001. *Facing the Ocean: The Atlantic and its Peoples. 8000 BC - AD 1500.* Oxford: Oxford University Press.

—. 2002. *The Extraordinary Voyage of Pytheas the Greek.* London: Penguin Books.

Edwards, K.J., D. Borthwick, G. Cook, A.J. Dugmore, K.-A. Mairs, M.J. Church, I.A. Simpson & W.P. Adderley. submitted. Landscape change in eastern Suðuroy, Faroe Islands: a hypothesis-based approach to the determination of natural processes and human artifice. *Human Ecology.*

Ekrem, I. & L.B. Mortensen. 2003. *Historia Norwegie* (trans.) P. Fisher. Copenhagen: Museum Tusculanum Press, University of Copenhagen.

Fellows-Jensen, G. 1996. Language contact in Iceland: the evidence of names. In *Language Contact across the North Atlantic* (eds) P.S. Ureland & I. Clarkson. Tübingen, 115-24.

Fisher, I. 2001. *Early Medieval Sculpture in the West Highlands and Islands* (Monograph 1). Edinburgh: RCAHMS / SOC ANT SCOT.

—. 2002. Crosses in the Ocean: some *papar* sites and their sculpture. In *The Papar in the North Atlantic: Environment and History. Proceedings of the St. Andrews Dark Age Conference, 2002* (ed.) B. Crawford. St Andrews, 39-58.

Forbes, A.R. 1923. *Place-names of Skye and Adjacent Islands: With Lore, Mythical, Traditional and Historical*. Paisley.

Friðriksson, S. 1982. Papey eða lundey. *Árbók hins íslenzka fornleifafélags*, 176-80.

Gammeltoft, P. 2001. *The Place-name Element in Old Norse bólstaðr in the North Atlantic area* (Navnestudier 38). Copenhagen: C A Reitzels Forlag A/S.

—. 2003. Contact or conflict? What can we learn from the island-names of the Northern Isles? In *Scandinavia and Europe 800-1350: Contact, Conflict, and Coexistence* (eds) J. Adams & K. Holman. Belgium, 89-97.

—. 2004a. Scandinavian-Gaelic contacts. Can place-names and place-name elements be used as a source for contact-linguistic research? *NOWELE* **44 (March)**, 51-90.

—. 2004b. Among *Dímons* and *Papeys*: What kind of contact do the names really point to? *Northern Studies* **38**, 31-49.

Historia. From editions and translations by Ekrem & Mortensen 2003 and Phelpstead 2001.

Íslendingabók. Edited by Benediktsson 1968.

Jonsson, L. 1999. *Birds of Europe with North Africa and the Middle East, with Illustrations by Magnus Ullman* (trans.) D. Christie. London: Christopher Helm A&C Black.

Keillar, I. 1994. *NORTH EAST STUDIES: Names in North-East Scotland. Project. Place-names and Settlement Patterns in Part of the Laich of Moray*.

Kruse, A. in press. Explorers, raiders and settlers: The Norse impact upon Hebridean place-names. In *Cultural contacts in the North Atlantic Region* (eds) P. Gammeltoft, C. Hough & J. Waugh.

Lamb, R. 1995. Papil, Picts and Papar. In *Northern Isles Connections: Essays from Orkney and Shetland presented to Per Sveaas Andersen* (ed.) B. Crawford. Kirkwall: The Orkney Press, 9-27.

Landnámabók. Edited by Benediktsson 1968.

Lowe, C. 2002. The *papar* and Papa Stronsay: 8th-century reality of 12th-century myth? In *The Papar in the North Atlantic: Environment and History. The Proceedings of a day conference held on 24th February 2001. The 'Papar' Project. Volume 1.* (ed.) B. Crawford. St Andrews: The Committee for Dark Age Studies, University of St Andrews, 83-95.

MacDonald, A. 1977. Old Norse *Papar* names in N and W Scotland: A summary. In *Studies in Celtic Survival* (ed.) L. Laing. British Archaeological Reports 37. Oxford, 107-11.

—. 2002. The *papar* and some problems: A brief review. In *The Papar in the North Atlantic: Environment and History. The Proceedings of a day conference held on 24th February 2001. The 'Papar' Project. Volume 1.* (ed.) B. Crawford. St Andrews: The Committee for Dark Age Studies, University of St Andrews, 13-30.

Mackintosh, H.B. 1928. *The Lossie and the Loch of Spynie*.

Matras, C. 1934. Papýli í Føroyum. *Varðin* **14**, 185-7.

O'Loughlin, T. 1999. Distant islands: the topography of holiness in the *Nauigatio sancti Brendani*. In *The Medieval Mystical Tradition: England, Ireland and Wales. Exeter Symposium VI. Papers read at Charney Manor, July 1999* (ed.) M. Glasscoe. Woodbridge: D S Brewer, 1-20.

Pálsson, H. 1955. Minnisgreinar um Papa. *Saga: Tímarit sögufélags* **5**, 112-22.

Pálsson, H. & P. Edwards (eds & trans.) 1972. *The Book of Settlements. Landnámabók.* Manitoba.

Peacock, J.D. 1968. *Geology of the Elgin District.* Edinburgh.

Phelpstead, C. (ed. & D. Kunin) 2001. *A History of Norway and The Passion and Miracles of the Blessed Óláfr* (Text Series XIII). London: Viking Society for Northern Research.

Ross, S. 1987. The submerged forest in Burghead Bay. In *MFC* (ed.) Bull.

Sandnes, B. 2003. *Fra Starafell til Starling Hill. Dannelse og utvikling av norrøne stedsnavn på Orknøyene.* Trondheim.

Schrœter, J.H. 1849-51. Færœiske Folkesagn. *Antikvarisk Tiddsskrift.*

Sharpe, R. (ed. & trans.) 1995. *Adomnan of Iona: Life of St Columba.* St Ives.

Simpson, I. & E.B. Guttman. 2002. Transitions in early arable land management in the Northern Isles - the *papar* as agricultural innovators? In *The Papar in the North Atlantic: Environment and History. The Proceedings of a day conference held on 24th February 2001. The 'Papar' Project. Volume 1.* (ed.) B. Crawford. St Andrews: The Committee for Dark Age Studies, University of St Andrews, 59-67.

Smith, A. 1842. Addition to the account of Holme and Paplay. In *The New Statistical Account of Scotland 15 (Orkney).* Edinburgh.

Stahl, A.B. 1999. Place-names of Barra in the Outer Hebrides. Unpublished PhD: University of Edinburgh.

Storm, G. (ed.) 1880. *Monumenta historica Norvegiæ. Latinske kildeskrifter til Norges historie i middelalderen.* Kristiania.

Sveinbjarnardóttir, G. 1972. Ritgerð til B.A.-prófs í sagnfræði í janúar 1972. *Mími* **19**, 1-20.

—. 2002. The question of *papar* in Iceland. In *The Papar in the North Atlantic: Environment and History. The Proceedings of a day conference held on 24th February 2001. The 'Papar' Project. Volume 1.* (ed.) B. Crawford. St Andrews: The Committee for Dark Age Studies, University of St Andrews, 97-106.

Taylor, S. 2002. *Unpublished Report:Report on comparative study of settlement place-names. Papar project.*

Thors, C.-E. 1957. *Den kristna terminologian i fornsvenskan.* Helsingfors.

Tierney, J. (ed. & trans.) 1967. *Dicuili: Liber de mensura orbis terrae.* Dublin.

Wainwright, F.T. 1962. *Archaeology and Place-Names and History: An Essay on Problems of Co-ordination.* London: Routledge & Kegan Paul.

Weidensaul, S. 1999. *Living on the Wind: Across the Hemisphere with Migratory Birds.* New York: North Point Press (A division of Farrar, Strauss and Giroux).

Wilson, D. 1851. *The Archaeology and Prehistoric Annals of Scotland.* Edinburgh.

Wooding, J.M. 2000. Monastic voyaging and the *Navigatio.* In *The Otherworld Voyage in Early Irish Literature* (ed.) J.M. Wooding. Dublin: Four Courts Press, 226-45.

Young, R. 1871. *The Parish of Spynie.* Elgin.

www.ingramcontent.com/pod-product-compliance
Lightning Source LLC
Chambersburg PA
CBHW061549010526
44115CB00023B/2991